THE GREAT CHICAGO BAR & SALOON GUIDE

To Jim,

without whom's
help I never could
of written it at
all.   love,

Dennis

THE GREAT CHICAGO BAR & SALOON GUIDE

CHICAGO'S 200 BEST BARS

Dennis B. McCarthy

Chicago Review Press

First Edition
First Printing 1978

ISBN 0-914090-46-1

Library of Congress Catalog Number 77-93721

Cover design and typography by Siemens
Communication Graphics

Published by
Chicago Review Press, Incorporated
215 West Ohio Street
Chicago, Illinois 60610

Preface

What we have here is a matter of aesthetics. Furious debate can be stirred among the drinkers of Chicago when the "best" or "better" bar issue is brought up. You can hear tavern orators give rhapsodic, impassioned speeches (punctuated by fists pounding bartops), about why one place will give you perfect drinking harmony while in another stray dogs wouldn't want to lap water.

I have boldly entered the fray of this debate and present you with a listing of over 200 of the best places to get a drink in the city of Chicago. In doing so I have avoided the zero-to-four stars rating system, or anything like it. How can you compare the Pump Room and the Baby Doll Polka Lounge on the same scale? I have given each bar its own explanation, let it tell its own story.

The best drinking pleasures in Chicago are often tucked away, if not hidden. You will find a vast range of drinking experiences in this city, just about one for every known taste. But a great part of the drinking story here is to be found in the neighborhoods, where, as often as not, there is a Ma-and-Pa tavern on every corner. For this reason, much of Chicago's bar culture seems to be hiding in the many little villages, each with its own borders, ways and laws, that make up the neighborhoods of the city. Go out and explore Chicago and its bars and you will be happily rewarded, as long as you don't wear a top hat, argue politics with a precinct captain or disagree with the bartender. In a doubtful situation, a generous tip will allow you almost any reasonable foible.

The bars listed here are "safe", in the sense that anyplace is. At the publisher's sensible request, I have not presented any bars in which, despite their other charms, there is any significant degree of danger. Common sense prevails. As it's said around town, you don't go in a bar that has bodies being tossed out of the door.

My credentials for this book probably began when I was christened Dennis Brian McCarthy on the South Side of Chicago. I learned about the ways of bars when my father would take me as a tyke into the local tavern on Saturday afternoons. There, with the excuse of being busy on manly hardware store-type chores, we would sit and sip. He had his beer, and I was filled to the tonsils with orange soda. The other customers would jam my pockets with candies and gumballs purchased from the backbar treasure horde, and they would pat me on the back and comment that I was a fine lad. It was then that I decided, despite the peculiar yeasty smell, that I liked bars.

Since that time, I've been to countless bars in Chicago and in other cities and countries. It's my proud distinction that I've only been thrown out of one bar in my life, and that was in Paris. I've been a bartender and a bar manager, and this book is the rather inevitable linking of two areas of my life: writing and drinking.

In preparing THE GREAT CHICAGO BAR AND SALOON GUIDE, I visited over 500 drinking and eating places in the city with one idea in mind: to select the best the city has to offer in a good drink and a good time. Some of the bars are obvious front yard tourist attractions, a few are rare and unusual hidden treasures. But in every case, I've tried to include bars that will be interesting, stimulating and soothing in their special ways. For variety and even a surprise or two, the selection of some saloons was on a capricious whim, and there were occasional nights of accidental drunkeness in which I found myself wandering, turning down unknown streets and entering strange, forbidding doorways. I consulted with bar owners, bartenders, drinkers and friends, and this book is a result of my search. You may not find your favorite watering hole here, and there are more than a few of the "name" places which are not included. I had a variety of reasons for this. Some are as vague as an aesthetic "wrongness" about the bar's atmosphere, some are as simple as the fact that they are lousy bars by anybody's standards.

Here are over 200 of the city's finest awaiting your investigation. Enjoy yourself. Belly up to the bar, have a cool one and toast the crazy city of the wild onion. Cheers!

Dennis B. McCarthy
Chicago
1978

Some Facts

• The selections are my own. No one paid to get in.
• Each bar is listed by name, address, the name of the proprietor or proprietress, and phone number. My comments follow, and then a series of cryptic symbols representing basic information which I gathered on my tour, listed in the following order:

—times of opening and closing.
—pricing: ¢ = cheap, $ = average, and $$ = expensive. This is a very subjective analysis based on what you get vaguely balanced against where you are. So, it is possible for two places to charge the same prices and one would be cheap (if, for example, tuxedoed attendants served you in a chaise lounge) and another would be rated expensive (if you have to sit on a beer keg as you drink champagne from the bottle).
—price of cheapest domestic beer/price of an average mixed drink, such as a vodka tonic.
—hours (#) of a lower-priced cocktail hour, if any.
—number of wines on the wine list and their price range, if any.
—number of domestic beers/number of imported beers.
—number and types of games available (as much for those who want to avoid them as for those who seek them out).
—type of music.

All put together, it looks like this:

11am-2am, $, 75¢/$1.25, # 4-7, 12 wines, $5-$15, 5 dom/3 imp, pinball, juke.

Sometimes all of this information was available, sometimes none of it was. One bar owner wouldn't tell me his name, the prices, or the hours, and went so far as to deny that he was really in existence. The philosophical implications of that were too much for me, so I left shaking my head. However, I've tried to give you enough information so that entering one of these joints won't be a surprise.

• This is my city, and in many ways it's beautiful, exciting and useful. Give it a try. Carry on.

x

This book is dedicated to Steve Cunneen, a saloon-keeper who maintains the Chicago tradition of lunacy and humor in a business that makes heads spin.

And thanks to those who helped:

Mary Barron
Richard Bresden
Eva Field
Art Gould
Mary Grant
Jim Hawking

Bob Hynes
Tim Hynes
Wayne Karjala
Cyril Landise
Gary Martin
Jim O'Connor
Bill Pletke

Acorn on Oak

116 E. Oak St.   944-6835
Tony Cangas, prop.

At the Acorn on Oak you can sit at the bar and listen to
the piano player swing through George Gershwin tunes,
songs from Irving Berlin, Cole Porter and Al Jolson, plus
a dash of jazz. For 7 years Buddy Charles has been the
Acorn's resident pianist, playing from 10 at night till 4 in
the morning, and he's become a Chicago tradition.

The Acorn menu offers a few Italian dishes, and the
usual burgers and bar-type sandwiches. The atmosphere
is den-like, with ships and paintings hung about. But
primarily, it's an intimate showcase for Charles' tunes
from the past.

11:30-4am, $, $1.00/$1.00, 1 dom/1 imp, piano 10-4am.

Adolph's

1045 N. Rush St.   337-7313
Fortune Renucci, prop.

Adolph's is a taste of 40's elegance. The bar curves in
deco-like fashion, wrapping itself around a piano at one
end. The bartenders wear vests, white shirts and ties.
The back-bar glistens, cocktail glasses are chilled on
crushed ice. At the rear is the restaurant, with Grecian-
like pillars and plastic floral groupings. There is, of
course, a coatroom.

Adolph's has been around for 47 years, and was remodeled in 1954. As the manager explained, "Everybody has come in here." Celebrities are often seen, and
sometimes you'll find an unexpected star jamming on the
piano. A great Chicago bar.

5pm-4am, $, $1.25/$1.50, no #, wine list, 6 dom/5 imp,
piano bar and strollers.

2

The Old Town Alehouse

219 W. North Ave.   944-7020
Elizabeth Thompson and Lucy Grider

For the sensible person or the serious drinker, Old Town has less to offer than it used to, but there are a few places worth recommending: The Old Town Alehouse, the Earl of Old Town, Second City, Orsi's and O'Rourkes. They're all within pub crawling distance of each other, which is fortunate because parking in so tight in the Old Town Triangle area.

The Alehouse is an Old Town oldie, since 1958. Then it was housed in the building across the street to the west of where it is now and owned by Eric Van Gelder who currently has the John Barleycorn Memorial Pub further north on Lincoln Avenue. In 1958 The Alehouse was a classical music, bohemian headquarters. A fire caused the operation to close down. The move after the fire was supposed to be temporary and the place was put together in a slapdash manner. Well, a third move never occurred and the Alehouse still looks ramshackle. There's a huge mural, done by Maureen Munson, which includes dozens of faces of the regular customers. There's a free library in the rear which operates on a take-one-leave-one basis.

The Alehouse clientele is a curious mixture of folks, indeed. Old Town residents drink here, so you'll find artists, writers, the Second City theater people, old men, dogs, housewives, all-in-all a pleasant and interesting blend of humans. It has a 4 o'clock license so often the place slides towards dawn getting looser, louder and crazier. You'll hear a harmless argument, roars of laughter, the reliving of stage experiences, general bedlam. And if you're lucky, maybe you'll be here late one night when Jim Belushi, of Second City's resident company, is around. If the "Theme from Rocky" comes up on the juke box, he springs up from his seat, runs up and down the bar throwing punches at the air, spars with a confused drunk who snarls, he moves on, flexing his muscles, waving to the cheering crowd, pauses to do a quick dozen push-ups on the bar floor, he's up again, throwing punches, waving, out the door to spar with the sky, ah yes, doing the Alehouse rock.

noon-4am, ¢, 60¢/$1.00, no # 3 dom/4 imp, pinball electronic, mixed juke box.

Alfie's

900 N. Rush St.   822-0300
Dan Reilly, prop.

On the Rush Street "miracle mile" lies Alfie's, a gay men's bar. It's a nice, well designed place with a split emphasis between a disco floor and conversational tables. One of the better aspects of Reilly's places (he also owns the Brownstone and Le Pub) is the absence of a dress code. In a comparable straight disco bar you'd find a couple of heavies at the door scrutinizing your coveralls and scowling at your turban. In Alfie's the nattily dressed businessman stands next to someone in shorts in a rather elegant atmosphere.

There's a heavy cocktail hour at Alfie's, from 4 till 8, and on Mondays it's jammed, all drinks are 75c. There are occasional gay benefits here, and there's a celebrity or two to be seen now and then. You'll find dark wood, books on shelves, paintings, wall hangings, and a cosy and elegant place for gay men to drink.

4pm-4am, $, $1.25/$1.50, # 4-8, 3 dom, disco.

Arnie's

1030 N. State in the Newberry Plaza   266-4800
Arnold Morton, prop.

Across the lobby from Arnie's is Zorine's, the newist elite private club in the city. It's at Zorine's that the latest in designer-fashion dining and drinking goes on. The masses, those who are not members of Zorine's, go right next door to Arnie's, which is Chicago's current leader in high fashion bars. Neither bar in the Newberry Plaza is even remotely related to the ordinary Chicago tavern scene.

As the manager put it, for some people Arnie's is "the place to see and be seen." The patrons are Chicago's Rush Street/Gold Coast Beautfiul People. The waitresses here are fashion plates. Arnie, who is described as an insatiable collector, has filled the place with a grandiose heap of antiques, art and *objets d'art*. In the brass-stained-glass-mirror-plant-sculpture battle of design elegance currently being waged in the dining and drinking places of the city, Arnie's has the edge by the sheer weight of its collections.

There are three rooms full of things to look at, while you eat, drink or dance. The dining room is huge and elegant, with a massive stained glass ceiling. The bar itself is square, with a small dance floor and a (ugh) mirror-covered piano. Sofas are against the walls and candles light the tables. The floor, of course, is carpeted. My favorite area is the garden room, which faces a wall of windows overlooking a small jungle in the central courtyard of the building. Trees, plants, flowers and water abound in the garden, and carousel horses hang in the air in the garden room, which is a drinking area till 7pm, then it's reserved for dining. A free chili-cheese bar is served to drinkers here from 5 to 10 pm.

In the midst of the art deco and art nouveau visual assault, you can see a beautiful antique juke box.

11:30-2, $$, $1.75/$1.75, # 11:30-4, 75 wines $4.50-175, 1 dom/limp, dinner dancing music Tues-Sat, 6-midnight.

Arnie's Sidewalk Cafe

1030 N. State   266-4800
Arnold Morton, prop.

On State Street, in front of the Newberry Plaza, which houses Arnie's and Zorine's, you will find Arnie's sidewalk cafe. It is a simple glass box with a bar, tables and a few plants. The major activity is people watching in the great Rush Street area stroll, and you can't beat four glass walls for that. Closed in winter.

M-F 12:30-1:30, Sat 10:30am, Sun noon, $, $1.00/$1.50, 1 dom/0 imp.

BBC

9 W. Division, second floor
Doug Buffone, prop.

Chicago Bear line-backer, Doug Buffone, owns BBC and it's the semi-dressy adult disco of Chicago. It's one of the original brass-antiques-plants places, and is the place to go if you are interested in fashionable disco dancing. There's a d.j. playing the music and a large dance floor flanked by one of the greatest, largest mirrors in the city. The mirror was reclaimed from an old mansion on State Parkway.

The BBC is large, there are two levels and a wall of windows to the front that face Division Street. The patrons are well dressed and fashionable. On a given night, for example, half the men will be wearing coats and ties, the other half in something like dress shirts and slacks. On Friday and Saturday nights there may be a wait of up to 30 minutes to even get in the place. If that happens, you can hole up in any number of places nearby, including Hotspurs on the first floor, which is a gussied up cafeteria that serves drinks. The BBC is a late licensed place, so if you need some fashionable disco till 4am, here's where you go.

8pm-4am, $$, $2/$2, 2 dom/1 imp, disco.

Baby Doll Polka Club

7315 S. Western Ave.   778-4778
Eddie Korosa, prop.

Here it is, Chicago's penultimate polka bar. The Baby Doll is one of the hugest bars I have seen. It looks like a big church basement with a sacrilegious bar running along one side of it. Long rows of tables run to the rear, interrupted by a dance floor. The tables have table cloths and candles. The place is ready for the polka.

The art deco bar could be an entrant in the city's longest bar contest.

Mr. Korosa, the proprietor, is a musician, and he's often on stage when the live music is performed on Friday, Saturday and Sunday nights, when the action starts. Every Sunday from 5-6pm WPOA am (1490) broadcasts a live polka performance directly from the Baby Doll. During the week it acts as a neighborhood tavern.

If you want to journey to Marquette Park, this is a highlight there, and if you've never heard Lil Wally, Chicago's king of polka, this is one of the places he can be found.

5pm-2, $, $1/$1, # 5-9, 12 dom/1 imp, live polka 3 nights.

The Back Room

1007 N. Rush St.   944-2132
Bob Hackett, prop.

Somewhere in the last couple of decades most of the old jazz clubs died and disappeared. While The Back Room isn't that old (11 years) it has preserved the flavor of the traditional Chicago jazz bars.

To find The Back Room, leave Rush Street and walk down the red carpet of a long forbidding gangway, whose walls are also painted red. When you get inside you stand in what was once a horse barn, then a garage. Now it's a tiny 2-story jazz club. The band is jammed into a far corner, and there's a bar built around the stage. People are ensconced in corners, and there's a dark blue layer of smoke at eye level. Blue jeans clad patrons sit next to couples in full evening dress, for all that matters is the music. The room is crowded, funky, tight and sub-terranean, everything a jazz club should be. Judy

Roberts plays here often, as do other name bands. The upstairs room is quiet and not much used.

Live music is performed seven nights a week.

4pm-4am, $, $1.50/$2.00/$2.00 cover, # 4-9, 2 dom, live music usually jazz.

The Bar Association

1224 W. Webster   871-1440

Tucked away on Webster is the Bar Association, one of those places that shuns advertising and prefers anonymity. It's primarily a restaurant, with a number of Persian dishes, and the tables are reserved for diners. But the bar is dark and beautiful. Sombre, nearly black wood was carved to create an impressive back bar. The bar top is covered with beautiful tiles, and a designed elegance fills the room. In the off-hours, when the restaurant isn't filled, it's a good hideaway, a place to retreat and have some privacy. It is expensive, though, and at dinner hour, especially on the weekends, it may be too crowded to be comfortable.

11:30-12:30am, $$.

The Bar of the Ritz and The Terrace

160 E. Pearson   266-1000
12th floor of the Ritz Carlton
Marban Corp., prop.

On the same floor as the Greenhouse you'll find The Bar and The Terrace, both owned by the Ritz Carlton. The Bar is a traditional night club with live entertainment. The Danny Long Trio is the house group and other acts are booked regularly. The place is dark, with a simple design and an emphasis on the performance area. Swivel leatherette seats and somber curtained walls are there for your pleasure. Generally, it's a traditional American club scene playing traditional popular music.

Of more interest is The Terrace which is a small fantasy garden in the manner of the Ritz. Wrought iron gates surround a pool of water with a fountain. Garden tables are set among trees, and there's a small island on which musicians perform after 6pm. Glass top tables and ice cream parlor chairs continue the garden look. A buffet lunch is served, then a buffet tea with drinks in the late afternoon, and cocktails and dancing are the word in the evening. It's certainly a long way from a lean-against-the-bar tavern, but there's something to be said for listening to a cello and piano over the tinkle of water in a man-made garden 12 stories above the city. A perfect place for lovers or your grandmother's birthday party.

1am-12, $, $1.50/$2, wine list, 1 dom/2 imp, live music.

Bar RR Western Cocktail Lounge

56 W. Madison   263-8207
Bill Goldstein, prop.

Knives, small cannons, reward posters, animal skulls, horns, sombreros, rebel flags, leather maps, Indian rugs, saddle, branding irons, a Victrola and one of the most impressive antique gun collections in existence. It sounds like a museum in Tucson but it's all in a bar in Chicago. Now where will you find this place? In the heart of the Loop, smack dab across from the First National Bank Building, down one forbidding flight of stairs. If you in our city for one convention weekend, you must drop in the Bar RR, for it is one of many proofs that the best of Chicago is not on the surface.

It's a downtown place, with a booming lunch crowd, lots of afternoon drinkers and a weird mixture of citizens rubbing elbows. Country music types favor the place, as do a good number of lawyers. At 8:30 the Sundowners perform live country music till 3:30am, 7 nights a week (don't ask me how they do it). The total impression is very western, very strange for where it is, but you'll enjoy yourself.

The gun collection is especially impressive. You'll see rows of items such as the Colt "Frontier", a .41 caliber gunfighter's pistol of the 1870's, and the "Pepper Box" revolver from the 1840's. I always took those disguised derringers in the movies to be a bit of Hollywood fancy, but the gun manufacturers of the last century were quite creative in their design of lethal objects. The Bar RR displays pistols disguised as pipes, canes and watches in its collection.

The food is "ranch style", of course, and it includes 30 chili items from basic chili through chili cheese tamale bowl to the ultimate (get ready) chili mac tamale cheese salami bowl. They even put perch in chili.

If you're downtown and need a drink in a western atmosphere, drop down to the Bar RR. They're open from 7am til 4am, and there are swinging doors into the men's room.

7am-4am, $, $1.25/$1.50, # 7am-8:30pm, 6 dom/1 imp, c/w live music 7 nights.

Barbarossa

1117 N. Dearborn   751-0624
Nancy Dauw, prop.

The Barbarossa is hidden inside a building that rests inconspicuously on a quiet side of Dearborn, just off the Rush Street area. From the front it looks like what it is, a small residential hotel, but once inside the doors you turn to the right and enter one of Chicago's best folk music clubs. Barbarossa is one of the city's oldest folk rooms, having been around for a decade, and it's a comfortable place to drink and listen. You can pick up a monthly schedule at the door and read the listings for future performances. Weekends are reserved for known Chicago talent, while newcomers play on weekdays. Tuesdays is an open mike night, and it's often better than you'd expect. If you want to hear ballads as sung by Jim Dooley, or by the likes of Jim and Vivian Craig, this is the place.

There are two levels here, and I like the ground floor better. The smoke drifts up to the second level, and you have to wait for the waitress to struggle upstairs with your drinks. Here it's seven nights a week, live folk music, local artists only. No cover.

4pm-4am, $, $1/$1.50, # 4-8, 3 dom/1 imp, live folk music, seven nights.

Barney's Market Club

741 W. Randolph   372-6466
Harry Schimmer

The menu describes Barney's as having survived "infamy, gangsters, police and Prohibition entanglements to become that quaint little restaurant on the wrong side of the Kennedy expressway," and it does have a bit of history.

The first Berghoff bar was in this building, then it was a florist's, a vegetable wholesale house, and 55 years ago Barney Kessel opened up his saloon and restaurant. Barney was quite a character, during Prohibition he made beer and whiskey in the bathtub and sold it across the bar. In 1929 he was sentenced to 60 days for bootlegging. During these 60 days, in fine Chicago style, the sheriff let him out over 40 times, though the sheriff hotly denied that, "Twasn't more than twenty."

Today you are greeted with a cheery, "Yes, sir, Senator" by the host as you walk in. This is Barney's trademark, hailing back to the days when Senators did stroll in. The bar is sedate, nearly sombre. Dark, quiet and old. The bartenders wear shirts and ties.

Half a block east is the site of Haymarket Square. A bit beyond that is Crane's alley, between Randolph and Washington off Desplaines. This is where an unidentified anarchist threw the bomb that killed 7 Chicago policemen and triggered one of the most tense stages of the labor wars in American history.

To the west on Randolph Street you'll find the Randolph Street vegetable market, so if you eat or drink lunch at Barney's you can stop at the stalls and buy fruits, vegetables and cheese at nearly wholesale prices.

Because of its location, Barney's is hardly a neighborhood place and you'll have to travel to it, but one advantage is that it's just a short jaunt from anywhere downtown by cab or car, and it's also possible to walk.

11am-11pm, $, 70¢/$1.00, 10 dom/2 imp.

The Baron's Lounge & Disco

4535 N. Lincoln Ave.   275-2680
Klaus K. Goerlich

Just Northwest in the city on Lincoln Avenue, you will find the improbable Baron's, a multi-purpose private club (your first visit is free, after that the membership fee is $50.) The bar is a multiple-reflection mirror box. It glistens and shines with disco glamour. The front room is science fiction modern, the rear is a disco dance floor framed by a mirror, the sound system is overpowering, and 400 people can crowd in here.

For club members, there are fashion shows at lunch, private meeting rooms on the second floor, club vacations, ski trips, dance lessons, movies, cartoons and home Bear games. Future plans include a greenhouse beer garden, enlarged disco and outdoor cafe with food service. At the very least it's an impressive organizational effort by Mr. Goerlich.

Disc jockeys, strobes, lighting effects and the usual sensory madness fill the disco area, while the front bar is curiously calm and pleasant in spite of the mirrors. The patrons, of all ages, pour in from the surrounding neighborhoods, more than from the club areas of the city. There's a dress code (no cut-offs or T-shirts), which gives the place a casually elegant air.

Finally, believe it or not, they offer a special disco wedding deal on Sundays. The room is free, drinks are at a reduced price. So if you have the urge to shake your bootie down the aisle, call Baron's.

I was talking with Mr. Goerlich and looking around his disco place. He seemed a staid fellow and the establishment out of character for him. I guessed he had brought a defunct gay disco and converted it to Baron's. His answer taught me never to underestimate the Chicago saloon keeper. "It was my plumbing shop," he answered.

noon-2, $, 75¢/$1.25, # 12-9, some German wines, 2 dom/2 imp, pinball, foosball, disco.

Barton's

75 E. Wacker   263-5474

This is another of those places that would rather not be mentioned in this book, but my dedication to the Chicago drinker is greater than my respect for the management's wishes. Barton's is primarily a restaurant, with an American menu, salad bar, and a specialty appetizer, shrimp in a bowl. They don't want, evidently, packs of drinkers to mess things up.

The bar is small, it has all of six stools, and there are eight booths around the room which can be used for cocktailing in the restaurant off hours. The room is intimate, designed like a library, there are sofas, books on shelves (that no one, I'm sure, ever reads), and paintings here and there.

Dark wood abounds, old stained glass catches the eye, and you are given a sense of age and history. The net result is a somewhat classical, Chicago version of an English lord's drawing room. There's a back bar that's open Mon-Fri at lunch and during cocktail hour.

So, if you're involved in a bit of romance and need a hideaway downtown, give Barton's a try.

Mon-Fri 11am-midnight, Sat & Sun 4pm-midnight, $$, 15 wines $5.50-$12, 5 dom/1 imp.

The Baton

436 N. Clark   644-5269
Jim Flint, prop.

"Felicia proudly presents the most lavish female impersonator show in the world, Baton's international revue is tops in the nation." So the cards on the table will tell you.

The old burlesque era of female strippers seems to have died in Chicago, but the torch has been taken up by impersonators. Chicago's straight strip joints are usually terrible alcohol-less rip-offs, where near beer and carbonated grape juice is served to you by young lovelies who will stroke your thigh for about $10 per finger. The Baton is a show lounge, with 200 seats and a large, professional, well-lit stage. Men in elegant full blown formal Mae West costumes do lavish Las Vegas-style productions before appreciative audiences. On weekends eight impersonators do solo pieces and production numbers, much of it in the style of those 1940's musical pieces, a kind of minor scale Bugsby Berkely affair.

There's a tile top bar, a photo gallery of the performers, and a large show room. I was fortunate enough to be there on an evening when the cast was rehearsing for the Baton's ninth annual "Toys for Tots" benefit revue. Judy Garland one-two-three-FOUR dance pieces were interspersed with lines like "Don't you know the words to that song yet, you bitch?" I asked Jim Flint, who mc's the performances, if all kinds of people were welcome here. "Hell," he answered, "We're on the tourist bus circuit."

8pm-4am, $, $1.00/$1.50, 4 dom, juke, female impersonator revue. Show times: 10:30, 12:30, 2:30, Sundays 7, 9:30, 1:30. $2 cover Fri & Sat, 2 drink minimum.

Beowulf

2326 N. Clark   750-1774
Rich Lansing and Gene Ross, props.

This is one of those half-level down places that appeal to the mushroom aspect of the drinker's personality. Bars are often like mushroom cellars, and the bar stool was even fashioned in the shape of the mushroom to point out just this similarity. The Beowulf is dark, cosy, and has the aspect of a library about it. Books and cabinets line the walls, and a calm quiet prevails.

4 o'clock bars are difficult. Often you'll feel that you've stumbled into a Star Wars scene, and often your fellow drinkers will lose control of some parts of their brain

which can cause erratic, anti-social or harmful behavior. The Beowulf is a 4 o'clock bar where the worst aspects of drinking with people who've been at it for 6 or 8 hours is avoided. They keep the peace here, and you don't get the feeling that you're in a mental ward. Most of the patrons are Near Northers in the 25-35 year old range.

There's a nice outdoor courtyard, and you can window watch at ankle level.

2pm-4am (noon-4am summer), $, 60¢/$1.25, # 4-7, 2 dom/1 imp, pinball, electronic, juke.

The Berghoff Cafe

17 W. Adams   427-3170
The Berghoff Family, props.

Back in 1887 the Berghoff brewery was founded in Indiana. Grandfather Herman had come over in 1856, he then brought his brothers and a brewmaster from Dortmut to set up shop. They had a saloon tent here in Chicago for two years during the Columbian Exposition of 1893 and liked the city. He tried to get permission to found a brewery here but failed. In retaliation, Herman opened three saloons. One was at Madison and Clark, the second was at Randolph and Halsted in the building that now houses Barney's Market Club. The third and surviving saloon was at the southwest corner of State and Adams, right next door to the current Berghoff's.

During Prohibition the Berghoff family did a very un-Chicago-like thing. They did not run a speakeasy. Their brewery made beer and extracted the alcohol from it. Maybe that spurred their history of excellent, reasonably priced food.

Today, the Berghoff Cafe is one of the classical musts in the Chicago bar and saloon scene. It's a stand up bar with no stools or chairs, you either lean against the bar or against one of the chest-high tables jutting from the wall. The room is comforting in that turn of the century dark, wooden way. You know that mega-gallons of drink have been consumed here. The bartenders wear white shirts and ties. Your grandfather may well have drunk in a place like this. There are hand painted murals on the wooden paneling, stained glass, a curved bar with lots of wooden cabinets. Everything is perfect down to the brass rail. There's a cashier/tobacco counter with more cigars than you're likely to find in most drinking establishments.

Try the draft beer. At 60c a stein it's clearly one of the best buys in the city. It comes both light and dark (I prefer the dark) and it is tasty, cold and good. The Huber Brewery in Monroe, Wisconsin, brews it for them according to the Berghoff formula. Berghoff also serves their own whisky, either 8, 10, or 14 year old, and they buy it, from the mash on up, in Kentucky.

In my student days I walked into Berghoff's one summer day and talked my way into a coveted job as a waiter. I have tasted about everything they have to offer and I recommend the place highly. The best bargain is lunch in the restaurant (in the off hours 2-4pm or so) or a sandwich in the bar. There's a sandwich buffet in the barroom from 10:30 til 7pm (Sat til 5), where one of the carvers will create your sandwich (on excellent Berghoff bread, of course) for a very reasonable price. Get a sandwich, grab a beer and go to a counter table, wrapped in the warmth of history, to enjoy yourself.

The patrons are downtowners, mostly men, and a conservative quiet generally reigns.

The food is great. The beer is great. The house wine in great. In fact, everything about the place is top notch.

10:30-8:30 (7 on Sat) closed Sunday and holidays, ¢, 60¢/$1.10, nice wines, 2 dom/9 imp.

Best Liquors and Wine

2116 N. Clark

The old fellows who've run this Near North place for practically ever now find their lease in jeopardy of being revoked, so they didn't want to give me any particulars on their operation. I suggest you drop in here before it's too late. This is one of those tiny, mysterious places that says "neighborhood tavern" from every square inch. It's never empty, never full, and in a tiny space combines tavern, full scale liquor store, and junk food dispensary.

There are a dozen or so stools, two tiny tables, a tv, hard boiled eggs, and a team of old timers who filter in and out. There's a good French restaurant, Cafe Michel, right next door, and since they don't have a liquor license, Best Liquors provides the goods. It's a tradition to enter Michel's with a bottle of wine bought next door. Best keeps an adequate selection of beers and wines, plenty of it cooled in the back cooler, and all of it served quickly and with a friendly smile. Good luck, old timers.

Biddy Mulligan's

7644 N. Sheridan   761-6532
Wrenn Nelson, prop.

Up north near the Evanston border sits Biddy Mulligan's, a music bar which brings blues, jazz and some rock to that part of the world. It's a big rambling kind of place with slanted, beamed ceilings, a long two-sided bar, and bench tables against the walls. Young people abound, many of them from nearby Northwestern and Loyola universities. There are more darts boards here than in any other place in the city, and Biddy's sponsors a team that competes in the city's bar circuit. There's a darts/pinball room in the rear, and the main room is reserved for music and darts.

Biddy's is a straightforward place, it's relaxed, gives you a nice feeling and has no particular hustle. There's a $1 cover, $2 on weekends when the music is almost always blues.

The building has been a bar since the 30's, and it averaged about three different owners and businesses per year. Since Biddy's been in residence for four years, it hold the longevity record. Maybe it's the free popcorn.

5pm-2am, closed Mondays, $, 75c/$1.25, 1 dom/2 imp, darts, pinball, foosball, music at 9:30.

The Billy Goat Inn

430 N. Michigan Ave. (lower level)   222-1525
Sam Sianis, prop.

You may wonder why the Chicago Cubs haven't won a pennant since 1945, but I don't wonder. I know why. It's very simple. It started back in 1934 when William Sianis, a young Greek immigrant, opened a bar across the street from the Chicago Stadium. It was called the Lincoln bar. One day a truck was going by the place carrying a load of goats. One of them jumped out of the truck and Mr. Sianis took it in as a pet, for in the southern part of Greece, which was his home, goats were very plentiful. In 1934 he changed the name of his place to the Billy Goat Inn, and he always kept a goat as his barroom mascot. Over the years "Billy Goat" Sianis (who grew a goatee, of course) took his pet goats (one at a time) to ball games, conventions, events at the Stadium, on airplanes and trains. A man in this country, after all, does have his rights.

The dark day came, however, in 1945 when Mr. Sianis and his goat were expelled (kicked out of) Cubs Park during the World's Series. The Cubs lost. Sianis sent a cable to Wrigley: "Who smells now?" and the black curse of Billy Goat Sianis was put on the Cubs. It is said that Billy lifted his curse before his death in 1970 at the age of 76, but we know better. In 1972, Billy's nephew, Sam, who now runs the business, brought his goat to Cubs park in a limousine (of course) with a large sign: "Forget the past. Let me lead you to the pennant." They were refused entrance at all 4 gates. The Cubs, needless to say, got nowhere that year.

In 1974 Sam took the goat to Oakland where the A's were competing for the pennant. They were treated royally by Charles Finley, sat in a box seat and watched the A's take the pennant. In 1977, Mr. Veeck welcomed Sam and goat to White Sox Park. There they stepped out of a limousine at home plate and strolled to their box seats. But the Cubs? O, no. They keep the goat out, year after year, and where has it gotten them? Sam Sianis doesn't say that the Billy Goat curse is still on, but his eyes smolder when he talks about it, and the intelligent observer can only make one conclusion. Why the management of the Cubs hasn't made the same, simple conclusion is a mystery. Well, that's the true story of why the Cubs flub and we still have a bar to discuss.

The Billy Goat Inn is a Chicago landmark. It moved to its present subterranean position in 1964. To find it, get to the 400 block of North Michigan, go down the stairs and wander around the bowels of the city till you stumble on it. It was established by the man Mike Royko called "the city's greatest tavern keeper," and is essential for any student of Chicago drinking. The place is a big room, split in the middle with a food counter and grill. One side is the bar, the other, tables. The walls are covered with photos of celebrities, blown up news columns, signs, and paintings. Billy Goat started his career in the U.S. as a news boy, and he kept a fondness throughout his life for newspeople. The tavern, walking distance from Tribune Tower, the Wrigley Building and the Sun Times/Daily News building, is a hangout for reporters, printers and paper staff. It's around the corner from the somewhat elegant Riccardo's, and as a bartender from O'Rourke's put it: "There's two kinds of newspaper writers, the ones who go to the Billy Goat and those who go to Riccardo's. They have one thing in common, however. After they get stiff they come here to O'Rourke's for a fist fight."

6am-2am, ¢, 50¢/90¢, 3 dom/2 imp, no games, juke.

The Black Forest Restaurant

2636 N. Clark St.   Di8-7930
Rudolf Naebe

Across the street from McDonalds on Clark Street, you'll find the Black Forest and its dark, comfortable bar. It's one of the oldest (50 years) German restaurants in the city. There's an inexpensive lunch menu ($2-$3), and a vast dinner menu offering German-American food from turtle soup to strudel. But the bar is solid. Dark, huge beams cross the wooden ceiling, and a fake arbor covers

the bar itself. The back bar has a wall mural of the monumental Heidelberg tun, a 50,000 gallon wine cask that
still rests in the Heidelburg Castle wine cellar.

The Black Forest is a favorite of older people in the
neighborhood. There are a few regular customers who
remember when it opened, though their accounts on the
details of the place's history seem to differ. You can eat at
the bar and there's an extensive wine list. On Friday,
Saturday and Sunday nights there's an accordion-
piano duo. Finally, there is an admirable oil painting on
the rear wall, and since most bar art is junk, take a look
at it.

11:30-2, $, 60¢/$1,25, 45 wines $6-$13, 3 dom/5 imp.

The Blue & Gold

2455 N. Clark
P. & P. Masini & F. Milazo

This tavern in the high rent district has a tiny carry-out
counter for newspapers and package goods, and it's next
door to Frances' Food Shop, the city's famous
home-cooking-plate-dinner palace. It's a tradition to
carry out Frances' dinners (meat and choice of 3 side
dishes, filling, good and cheap) walk next door, have a
drink and watch the ball game. If you don't have a
mother who cooks for you, you can restore the tissues
and the psyche with Frances' food. It's a New York style
place, with a steam table set up and mounds of fresh,
good edibles.

The Blue and Gold has its separate integrity as a
small, traditional tavern with a hodgepodge of local citizens, but its relationship with Frances' makes a pleasant
wedding. During the evening hours, the place will fill
up, the working women stop in to get things from the
counter, kids come and go and several generations sit
side by side. There are a couple of old write-ups posted
that tell you the Blue & Gold history, the bartenders

wear aprons and it's another of those places that makes you wonder if it can survive the Northside's transition to hip, fast action.

7am-2am, ¢.

Boccaccio's Cantina and Market Deluxe

153 E. Erie   944-2450
Boccaccio's Inc., prop.

This is a newcomer to the land of North Michigan Avenue, and it's done with a comfortable sense of quality. There's a dining room and a deli room which has deli-style take out foods. The menu is Italian, as was Boccaccio a few years back, and there's a large sandwich menu available for lunch time.

The bar room is designed with a massive stained glass window behind the bar, curtained windows and a couple of stand up counters for the quick munch and sip at the noon hour. It's a pleasant enough room, and you can order appetizers at any time, including oysters, clams, garlic bread and pizza. As a newcomer, it's better and more tasteful than most, and there are nice touches, such as cappuccino served at the bar and the different but pleasing designs of each room.

11am-11pm, Fri & Sat till 12, Sun 4-10, $, $1.00/$1.50, 12 wines $4.50-$7.50, 1 dom/1 imp, tapes.

Booze & Bits

111 E. Oak St. (Coach house, rear)   751-9389
Leo Sweeney, prop.

This is one of the rare bars that I can recommend highly. Everyone in Chicago should visit Booze and Bits at least once. Imagine: you're haunting the Rush Street area in a daze. The environment has gotten to you, escape is essential, but you doubt that you have the fortitude to walk the 11 miles to the place where you found the closest parking spot. What to do? You turn down Oak Street, past the lights and the glare, past the impeccably dressed men and the women with perfect faces. At 111 East Oak, where this book told you to go for an honest drink, there is nothing. Booze & Bits is not there! But wait a minute. I haven't misled you. Look down at the sidewalk and you'll see an arrow. Follow it down a long, long gangway, and you may begin to chuckle, now that the end is near. The confusion of the street is blessedly far behind and ahead is a sumptuous reward.

Cross the threshold of Booze & Bits, and you find yourself in a cozy, two-level bar. It's converted from a coach house which has been there forever. The first floor is big enough for a dozen people, and the second floor, which has one table and some games, is where you would go to foment a conspiracy. How blissful, how calm. You can lean on the copper bar and gaze at the lovely cement and red brick design and know that you have arrived, because the beer you just ordered cost only 50 cents.

11am-2, ¢, 50c/$1, 1 dom/1 imp, games, juke.

Boul Mich

528 N. Michigan Ave. (around the walkway to the west)
Ron & Jerry Andrews, props.   644-0767, -0768

Boul Mich is a traditional stop on the Magnificent Mile. While most places located near Michigan Avenue have a limiting suit-and-tie pallor about them, the Boul Mich neatly combines irreverence and a definite saloon atmosphere so that the suit and tie are not combined with a stuffed shirt. Here, media executives, models, actors, newspaper people, and a regular crowd of anybodies drink happily together. The age group is mid-twenties through middle age.

The Boul is dark, borders on the dingy, and is often full of rowdy good times, especially in the late afternoons and early evenings, when the office workers drink away the daily tensions. You can find the drinkers gathered around the piano doing an off-key sing-a-long, or wandering around the room, meeting and greeting.

9am-4pm M-F, $, 75¢/$1.50, 3 dom/0 imp, juke & radio.

The Brassary

625 N. Michigan Ave.   266-2757
James Maccione, prop.

On the sublevel, beneath the Michigan Avenue side-walk, lies the Brassary. Here hordes of young, upwardly mobile, office-working Americans pile in for lunch and after work drinks. They have an outdoor cafe-bar that isn't too attractive, and the dining room is designed in fast-food bright colors, but if you stick near the bar it is a pleasant enough place. There're two walls of windows, lots of hard wood and plants hanging around. Wednesdays and Fridays are the big days here, and there is a disc jockey and dancing in the evening. Deli style food is served, and they have what is probably Michigan Avenue's only public house ping pong table.

11am-2am, $, 75c/$1.25, 1 dom/5 imp, pinball & ping pong, disco.

The Brewery

3144 N. Broadway   929-9773
George Badonsky, prop.

Tony Barone designs restaurants and bars, and he is responsible for a good number of what Mike Royko describes as "the swinging restaurants with cutesy-poo names." Here in the Brewery, Barone has done a job in a new, non-traditional way. The bar is curved and copper covered. Above it copper tubing spirals crazily from the ceiling to end with small spot lights. The walls are curved, there are ramps and sculptured table seating. The effect is clean, uncluttered and pleasing. The bar itself is small, but the restaurant tables can be used during off-hours. The food is eatable at a low price, and the salad bar is one of the best in the city. If you need a waitress, ask for Kathryn and tell her I sent you.

George Badonsky, the owner, is a wine connoisseur. He owns the Tango, which has a massive wine list, but here at the Brewery he has carefully picked 10 very good wines, and prices them at $4.50 to $5.00. There's also a host of specialty drinks, those fresh fruit sundaes that the traditional drinker will eschew, and free addictive sesame sticks to munch on.

If for no other reason, you'll want to go to the Brewery to sit in a building that was once an Al Capone hideout. Down in the basement there was a phone booth (communications) and escape tunnels (transport) for the Capone boys. Good times.

11:30am-midnight, $, 60¢/$1.25, 10 wines $4.50-$5, 3 dom/2 imp, pinball, juke and tapes.

Broadway Joe's

6036 N. Broadway   743-9465
Pat Lyons & Larry Swoboda

Broadway Joe's is your basic neighborhood tavern, with an emphasis on sports and a generally young crowd in the evenings. The place has been a tavern for over 50 years, and it's worn and battered as any place would be that's seen countless cases and thousands of drinkers go by. There's a certain satisfying feeling to those places that have cases stacked against the wall and floors that tilt as you go to the washroom. Broadway Joe's is such a bar. There are two tv's, a pool table, and pinball. The beer company claptrap is mounted on the walls and there are a couple of oddball tables for intimate drinking. Good sandwiches are served, you can get a glass of Heineken and the jukebox provides entertainment.

11:30-2, ¢, 65¢/80¢, # Fri. 4-7, 3 dom/1 imp, pool & pinball, juke.

The Brownstone

435 W. Diversey   472-0803
Dan Reilly, prop.

The building itself, a brownstone, is incredibly beautiful.
This 130 year-old mansion comes from an era of work-
manship that can't be met today. Now, it's penned in by a
hot dog stand, but it's well worth gazing at if you're
strolling past. Here, in the heart of the "gay ghetto," Dan
Reilly has opened his third gay men's bar. It's located
half a level down from the street and like Reilly's other
places, Le Pub and Alfie's, is done in a tasteful and
attractive way. Hard wood abounds, antique bevelled
glass panels shimmer, a dance floor and a comfortable
curved railing at the front window complement the
decorations, making this a classy place. There's a small
terrace in front with flowers and tables for use in clement
weather.

On the second floor of the Brownstone you'll find the
Living Room, a simply designed lounge and disco.

The music is disco, with a dj three nights a week. On
Tuesday all drinks are 75c.

4pm-4am, $1/$1.25, # 4-8 & all day Tuesday, 3 dom/
1 imp, no games, juke and disco.

The Bulls

1916 N. Lincoln Park West   337-6204
Lino Darchum, Jim Planey, props.

Founded in 1963, The Bulls is one of the grandfathers of
contemporary music clubs in the city. Vince Azzaro,
who started the Earl of Old Town in 1958, sold his interest in it and opened the Bulls. Your first visit to this
bar may be a bit shocking. It's in a type of sub-
basement with the decor of a neolithic cave. Acoustical
gunk rounds out the ceiling and walls to create the sub-
terranean effect. This club has a history of booking only
local, original talent and has the feeling of a neighborhood hangout, especially after 2am when the bar-

tenders, waitresses and musicians stroll in from the other places in town. Food is served, including the world-renowned Bulls taco.

In September of 1977 the present owners took the place over, and changed some policies and aspects of the interior. The groups that are booked now tend toward the quieter, more acoustical sound than before. In the old days you could get your ears acid-rocked in this cave, but things have mellowed. There's a new copper bar top and a lot of cleaning and behind the scenes activity that now gives you the impression that even if you're in a cave, at least it's a civilized one.

4pm-4am, $, 75¢/$1.25, # 4-9, 4 dom/2 imp, live music 7 nights.

Butch McGuire's

20 W. Division   337-9080
Butch McGuire, prop.

Butch McGuire's is the original, ultimate Chicago singles bar. It was opened in 1961, and McGuire says, "It took Chicago three or four years to figure the place out." It's housed in an early 20's terra cotta front building, which harks back to when Chicago was the nation's leading manufacturer of terra cotta, though there are very few buildings of its style left. The place was a speak-easy during the Hidden Years of Prohibition. Inside there's a slew of antiques and collector's items, many of them hung from the ceiling, since the walls have to be kept free for action, given the masses that come and go through here. The bartenders and floor men wear white shirts and McGuire green ties, and there are over 100 employees needed to staff the place. They form a rather dedicated club, half of them are college students, and you can always get a drink, regardless of the crowd.

Singles bars are for men and women to meet each other. I've heard this strip of Division Street called the "street of dreams," but McGuire has some astounding statistics about the mating that goes on here. "Over 2400 couples have met here and then gotten married. Just imagine the kids." There'll be an entire generation of McGuire-based children.

Everyone's been here. They pour in. It's often a little hard to believe. Ironically, McGuire has launched a national advertising campaign. For what, many people don't know.

10:30am-2am, $, 75¢/$1.25, # 10-8, 2 dom/5 imp, pinball, juke, fook 11am-3pm, 7 days.

The Cabaret, Act 2

3730 N. Clark   935-2900
Charles Renlow, prop.

This is the Center Stage's tastefully done Cabaret music room, and it has a bona fide natural spring right there in the corner. It's found in the basement of the recently purchased Northside Auditorium Building, beneath the Disco and the Victory Garden's Theatre. For years there had been leakage problems in the basement of the building, and no one knew quite what the problem was. A backed-up sewer? A cracked water main? Investigation by the present management discovered a little natural spring bubbling away right there in the corner, giving up water purer than the stuff we drink. Rather than fight the spring any longer, the Cabaret people cooperated with it by smashing out a section of floor, giving the spring free rein. They installed plants on the edges and a few goldfish, and they have what no other place in Chicago can claim, a gay cabaret with its own spring. The decor is tastefully done, with cocktail tables, carpeting and a designer bar. The Cabaret has a membership fee and a varying cover charge. It's one of the more elegant gay places in the city and offers a variety of cabaret entertainment from 9pm Wednesdays through Sundays.

7pm-4am, $, 75c/$1.25, 2 dom/1 imp, pinball, cabaret music.

Cafe Bohemia

138 S. Clinton   782-1826
James Janek, prop.

Most people go to the Cafe Bohemia as a place to eat, but the bar, not so well known as the restaurant, has its place in the drinker's universe. If you're at Union Station waiting while Amtrak scratches its head, cross the street to the northwest and visit the Cafe's bar. Set in a building that used to be a hotel, you'll find a quiet, traditional atmosphere. Dark wood, peanuts, a bartender with a shirt and tie, all these things reassure the jangled nerves.

As you sit at the bar, your back will be to the dining area, where the menu offers the flesh of several of our animal friends on the almost-endangered-species-list. Meat of lion, bear, moose, elk, deer, pheasant, and even hippo is served. There are heads on the walls and stuffed birds dangling in the air, so queasy vegetarians and bird-watchers beware. The wine list includes over 75 kinds ranging from $5.50 to $20.00. There's a limo service for diners to and from theatres and sporting events. Not bad for a cafe.

7am-midnight, $, $1.00/$1.50, 2 dom/2 imp, musak.

The Cape Cod Room

Arcade Level, Drake Hotel
Lake Shore Dr. & Michigan Ave.   SU7-2200
Drake Hotel, prop.

This annual-award-winning seafood restaurant is decorated so that you absolutely believe you're in a New England coastal inn. They have the appropriate artifacts hanging on the walls, dark, heavy beams cross fake windows that look to the sea, and red checked tablecloths cover the tables. The bar is small, it has stools for 9 and a little place where maybe 3 more people could stand. Next to it there's an even tinier oyster bar where shell fish are opened before your eyes. The bartenders wear white aprons, white shirts and ties, there's an aquarium over the back bar, and Drake Hotel elegance is to be found.

The bartop is an old tradition. It has about 2 million different carvings of initials and other vital data. Not long ago the management installed a new, finely finished bartop. The drinkers rebelled and won their cause, the old top was replaced. It's not often that you find a restaurant which is frequented by celebrities and gourmets, which also encourages people to carve their initials on the bar.

noon-midnight (food till 10:30), $$, 85c/$1.65, wine list, no music, jackets required.

The Celtic Lounge

10934 S. Western   233-8897
Frank Cunningham, prop.

The Celtic Lounge is an archetypical Southside third generation Irish neighborhood bar. They sport two TV's (you won't have to miss a game), and Bears and Notre Dame games are important events here. There's pinball, a bowling machine, and the usual tavern stuff is supplemented by that Erin go bragh Irish nonsense that people put on walls. Guinness and Harp are served, as well as sandwiches.

If you are visiting Chicago for only a short time you should jump in a cab and dash to the Celtic Lounge. It will only cost you 15 or 20 dollars and it will be a vital Chicago experience. If that seems extravagant, it's not. Do it. After all, Cunningham is my cousin and these things are important.

noon-2, ¢, 50¢/75¢, # noon-6, 6 dom/1 imp, juke.

Checkerboard Lounge

423 E. 43rd St.   373-5948
Buddy Guy, prop.

The Checkerboard Lounge is an unassuming little tavern on a commercial street. You enter into a barroom with a long curving bar, and go into the next storefront room, which is set up with two long banquet-style tables with white plastic tablecloths, something in the manner of a Polish wedding. The action here is Southside Black blues, with your host Buddy Guy doing a lot of the stage work with his brother Phil and their band. You can also see Junior Wells, Lefty Dizz and Nick and the Ghetto Kings here. There are a number of Southside blues places which draw visitors from other races and other parts of the city, but the Checkerboard is the most civilized, the most genial, and the one with the least racial tension. White folks, especially the young, used to do a lot of visiting at Ma Bea's on the west side, Theresa's and Peppers on the South Side, but the practice has been reduced since a number of places have followed the Wise Fool's lead and now book the same musicians on the North Side.

At the Checkerboard, up to half of the audience can be white on a given night, and most of them look like they've walked over from the University of Chicago. Travelers should be more paranoid about the street than the bar. Park as close as you can, even illegally, for it's not the kind of neighborhood where street-foolish people should be wandering. There's sometimes a $1 cover at the door, but not always. Feel welcome, have a good time.

noon-2am, $, live music Fri-Sun at 9pm, Monday at 5pm

Chicago Club of the Deaf

4221 W. Irving
The Club, prop.

Chicago has a few clubs where deaf people come to do
the same things everyone else does in a bar. The CCD is
the best of the bunch. The place is big, if not cavernous.
You'll find it to be more like a social club than a tavern,
in design and in its activity. They're only open from 6:30
pm till closing on Friday, Saturday and Sunday. The
place is brightly lit, which aids talking with sign language, and it's the kind of environment where the
members don't feel they have to drink when they're
there. Friday nights are film nights, with captions, the
second Saturday of the month is Bank Night, where cash
lottery-type prizes are handed out, and there are a
bunch of sports teams sponsored. It's a members club,
but deaf visitors are always welcome. If you know
someone who's deaf and is looking for a place to
socialize, direct them to CCD.

6:30-closing Fri., Sat., Sun. only, ¢, 60¢/75¢, 6 dom.

The Clark Street Cafe

2260 N. Clark   549-4037
Rob Goodrich, prop.

A newcomer to the Near North, the Clark Street Cafe is
Chicago's version of a San Francisco fern bar. The place
is split, half bar and half restaurant. Airy, high ceilings,
lots of hardwood furnishings and antiques, open
windows, stained glass mirrors, plants and statuary. The
Clark Street Cafe was designed, not thrown together.
The drinker is given a sense of comfort and elegance that
is almost un-Chicago in nature, but pleasant to experience. The clientele is fashionable, fashion conscious,
and naturals on the backgammon board. A good place to
go when you can't afford the air fare west.

4pm-2am, $, 65¢/$1.25, # 4-7, wine list in dining area, 4
dom/2 imp, backgammon, low key taped music.

Clearwater Saloon

3447 N. Lincoln   935-6545
Lerner Corp., prop.

This is a young people's music bar specializing in bluegrass, blues and country music. You'll find a
loose-towards-rowdy atmosphere with wall-to-wall
people drinking, stomping their feet and occasionally
yelling Yee-ha!

The place has two levels, bare brick walls and a
minimum-grungy decor. It's the kind of bar where a
table consists of a rough slab of wood on a stand and you
wonder if the toilets work. No one seems to mind,
however, and you can certainly feel comfortable.

There is no cover or minimum, but they do a rather
cornball pass-the-hat for the musicians routine after
each set.

4pm-2am, $, 65¢/$1.10, no #, 4 dom/4 imp, pool table
and pinball, live music seven nights.

Colette's

2515 N. Lincoln Ave.   477-5022
Michael Thomsen, prop.

Colette's is a very pleasant Chicago cafe-bar. It's a triangular two-story building, done in a white stucco with
lots of open windows, plants and a hint of privacy at the
small tables. During the day it's a quiet, conversational
place where you'll hear the occasional musician hit away
at the piano. At night it's a music bar featuring a variety
of groups, most of them doing traditional jazz.

One of the features of the place is determined by
Michael Thomsen, the proprietor, who believes in beer
but not in "fancy" drinks. You have an excellent choice
of over 30 imported beers which are not limited to any
particular region of the world, as they often are in ethnic
bars. On the other hand, you may have a hard time
getting a banshee here.

If you need a quiet place for a private chat in the evening, try Colette's. At night, be ready for a cafe music scene.

6pm-2am, $, $1/$1.25, # 6-9, 2 dom/30+ imp, no games, live music, often jazz.

The Coq d'Or

Arcade Level, Drake Hotel
Lake Shore Dr. & Michigan Ave.   SU7-2200
Drake Hotel, prop.

Coq d'or opened the day after Prohibition was repealed, and it was designed to recall the New England drinking rooms of the early 1800's. It's panelled in rich butternut and is a Chicago classic, the kind that's been patronized by the Queen of England and the Emperor of Japan. The atmosphere is one of civilized restraint, jackets are required after 5pm, and if you've had too many, coffee miraculously appears before you. There's a small luncheon menu served from noon til 3pm, and there are always nuts to munch on.

The hotel business has changed over the years. The Drake has been a symbol of elegance in Chicago for a long time. Once limousines rolled up, steamer trunks were carted in, chauffeurs and footmen were available for service, and, in a way, those were the days. Now conventioneers dominate the scene. The Coq d'Or still stands proudly, its dark and rich comfort is a soothing experience, and when you sit here, it's so quiet you can hear the ice cubes clink.

Mon-Thurs 9am-1am, Fri 9am-1:30, Sat 5-2, Sun 12-12, $$, 85¢/$1.65, wine list, no music.

Como Inn
The Caffe Pappagallo

546 N. Milwaukee Ave.   421-5222
Marchetti Family, prop.

The Como Inn is an incredible museum of Italian art-work, furniture, statuary, stuffed animals, furniture and decorative items. Entering the lobby is a surreal event, almost too much for the eye, like a crowded antique shop. Amidst the thirteen dining rooms and the halls with teams of gypsy-costumed service people, is one lounge, the Caffe Pappagallo. Pappagallo is "parrot" in Italian, and the room is decorated in a formal style with a dash of parrot art here and there. There's a piano in the center room, cafe seating along the walls, candles and flowers on the tables and a sense of foreign elegance. The menu here includes a wine list with 32 wines, appetizers such as clams, mussels, stuffed mushrooms and oysters, Italian desserts, and expresso and cappuccino coffees. This puts the Pappagallo in the true class of the caffe, where bottles of wine, snacks and good coffees are a tradition.

The Como Inn has weathered over 53 years of urban change, so that it now is surrounded by an industrial wasteland, and is flanked by an expressway. Don't worry about the surroundings, however, because there's valet parking and once you're inside you'll have no idea what part of the world you're in. Como is a lake in Italy that Mr. Marchetti fell in love with before he came to this country from Florence. The place is known for its constant expansion, change and remodelling. It's been an endless process over the years. This is another of the Chicago classics, and as such it was, naturally, a speak-easy in the Dark Times.

noon-midnight, $, $1.00/$1.75, 20 wines $4-$35, 6 dom/ 3 imp, piano.

The Cove

1750 E. 55th   684-1013
Dick O'Connell, prop.

When this place was the 1750, some years ago, it was a
Hyde Park old timers bar with a sense of frayed elegance. New owners have come in, redecorated, expanded into a second storefront, and attracted the U of C
student population. Many of the old timers have stayed
on, and there's a pleasant barroom intermingling between generations.

The bar and back bar are 1930's beauties, dark, art
deco, with columns, and there's a nice curve to the bar
itself. The new decor clashes, however, for they've
brought in nautical gear to make the Cove a cove. It's for
those who prefer carpeting and pinball to bar boards and
backgammon. The jazz juke box is popular.

10-2, $, 60¢/90¢, 3 dom/1 imp, pinball, jazz juke.

Crown Pub

O'Hare Hilton, promenade level
O'Hare Airport   686-8000
Hilton Hotels, prop.

If you are stuck (or lost) in O'Hare airport there are many
places to get a drink, but unfortunately most of them
can't be distinguished from cafeterias or laundromats. If
you want intrigue, you can hike to the lounge in the
International Building, and if the flights are moving,
you'll watch the strangest mixture of people Chicago has
to offer.

But if you're trying to escape the fact that you're in an
airport, go to the bowels of the Hilton Hotel (connected
to the terminal by a tunnel) and enter the Crown Pub. It's
an expensively furnished "olde" pub-style tavern. Dark
wood, English prints, and comfortable chairs are here to
help you relax. There's a simple menu, offering roast
beef and corned beef sandwiches, cheddar cheese soup,
Scotch eggs, potted shrimp and English trifle. The TV
and the fact that the bar is also a service bar for another

restaurant are the only distractions, but if you sit in a corner, you can forget that your flight was cancelled while your luggage was rerouted to Toledo, forget that you have to pass religious panhandlers in order to get anywhere and take a sip of your favorite drink.

10am-12:30, $, 90¢/$1.40, 40 wines, 7 dom/3 imp.

Cunneen's

1424 W. Devon   743-9196
Steve Cunneen, prop.

Cunneen's is Rogers Park's most active corner tavern. By day it is a pleasant neighborhood bar with large open windows and lots of plants; a good place to read a newspaper. You'll find the atmosphere has a South American bus effect: old folks, young folks, kids, dogs, people with groceries and laundry.

At night the young people pour in. Cunneen's formula is simple. By providing a pleasant environment, bottom-line prices, and a first rate stereo system which rocks at night, the place has cultivated a faithful clientele. You are at the mercy of the bartenders' taste when it comes to music, they play albums at their whim, so it may be any-thing from hard rock, to jazz, c/w or Perry Como. Chess, checkers and backgammon are popular, and you can get Chivas on the rocks, a bottle of Heineken, Guinness or Harp for $1.00. You can almost always count on a crowd at night, Cunneen's doesn't seem to know the dif-ference between Tuesday and Saturday nights. Mirac-ulously, there's no tv and no juke box.

Well, so much for objectivity. I've known Cunneen since before he opened this bar, and I've worked in it, off and on, over the years. Needless to say, my view is warped. At times it seems like a nice little tavern, often it strikes me as a rock and roll hell hole. Everything goes on here. For surreal zaniness, it is only surpassed by its next door neighbor, the Unameit. At two o'clock, the Cunneen's diehards stroll the long twenty feet to enter the Unameit, which its owner proudly describes as "semi-sleazy." Here you'll find smoke-blue air, the world's dirtiest and ugliest mirror, and a Star Wars cast

of nearly sentient drinkers. As one of the regulars
described it: "It has everything, if you're not choosy."

Noon-2am, ¢, 50¢/80¢, no #, some wines, 4 dom/5 imp,
pool table, an active stereo.

The Disco, Act 1

3730 N. Clark St.   935-2900
Charles Renlow, prop.

Bistro, watch out. Charles Renlow, one of the leaders of
the Chicago gay men's community, has bought the
Northside Auditorium Building and has remodelled and
installed a tremendous disco. The room is the theatre
used by the Victory Gardens Theatre Company, and
they've been moved up one flight to a smaller theatre.
The disco room is nicely restored and works with, rather
than violates, the integrity of the structure. There's a
huge dance floor, the best in sound and lighting systems,
and a screen covers the stage for 6 projectors, animated
slides, a special effects projector, and an incredible
laser light show. Loops of laser light leap about the air
with a three-dimensional effect. Globes, spotlights and
the rest of the usual disco effects are also present.
    The Disco is linked with the Cabaret, an entertainment
lounge in the basement of the same building, and they
are both part of Center Stage. There's a membership
policy for Center Stage, with a fee, and a cover charge
of $1.00 on Sun., Wed., and Thurs., $3 on Fri & Sat.
(drink included), and no cover for members on Monday
and Tuesday. Gay benefits and activities are occasionally held, and the entire operation looks like it's
going to be one of the classiest operations in the city.
Gay women are encouraged to give the place a try, and
they are welcome.

7-4, 75¢/$1.25, 2 dom/1 imp, pinball, disco.

The Domino Lounge

57 E. Walton   DE7-9416
Club Domino, prop.

As you walk in the door the piano player will probably
insult you, unless he's busy insulting someone in the
audience. Frank Remmy, known in some circles as Dirty
Frank, is the one-man continuous entertainment here.
He plays the piano, sings, cracks jokes, tell gags and
taunts the patrons. It's a slick, after hours place that gets
a lot of restaurant people after two, a run of middle-aged
conventioneers, the occasional celebrity, and other out
of towners. Professional singers drop in now and then,
and anyone is likely to wind up belting a tune, whether
they can sing or not.

It's found on the second floor, overlooking Walton
Street, small, lounge-like in decor, with red patterned
wallpaper, a large mirror and small stools for the
audience.

If you're a wit and want to match what you have
against Frank, give it a try. And good luck.

8pm-4am, $$, all drinks $2.50, # 9-10:30, 2 dom, Frank
from 9-4.

Dugan's Bistro

420 N. Dearborn   467-1878
Edward Davison, prop.

This is the gay boogie palace of Chicago. On a Saturday
night some 1500 people pass through its doors, most to
dance in a mad frenzy in a large disco room with super-
sonic speakers and every known lighting device. There
are three bars. The first is on the main floor, which is a
bar-lounge area with carpeted steps used as seating. Up
half a level is the dance floor, with one bar, and at the
rear you'll find a slightly quieter lounge area done in
mirrors and modern chrome furniture.

Everyone is welcome, and Davison estimates that
30-40% of his weekend patrons are straight. The Bistro
has been a fashionable place for the young and daring

straight people to go dancing. When you approach from the outside (which is purple with a yellow awning and therefore hard to miss) be ready to go through a thorough ID check regardless of your apparent age. Dugan's is very cautious and they require five ID's (a number I haven't had since I was 17). Once inside, it's boogie time. Don't bring your maiden aunt from Iowa, if she's upset by men who use the women's room and make out with each other. But it may be worth it, if she'll get to expand her consciousness watching the go-go boys swing. They are only topped by the great bearded lady, a heavy-set fellow with a beard who dresses in drag and dances. He wears something like eight dresses in varying styles and does a truly outrageous strip down to underwear or a bathing suit. All this is what used to be, years ago, Gus' Restaurant.

4pm-4am, $, 50¢/$1.25, # 4-7, 3 dom/1 imp, pool, pinball, disco & juke.

Durkin's

810 W. Diversey   525-2515
J. Olson, Z. Gac, & S. Mielczarek, props.

Before 1918 Durkin's was a restaurant, from 1918-1933 it was Prohibition Willy's Speakeasy. Since then, it's been named Durkin's. When the present owners were re-modelling in 1974 they stumbled on a secret room in the basement full of White Horse scotch and Portuguese brandy, without government seals, of course, and in pre-twist-top bottles.

Today you'll find a modern Chicago quasi-Irish design (benches from the wall, plants, antiques, stained glass, brick walls). The front bar room was the old restaurant, and the rear game room was the speakeasy.

By day it's a neighborhood bar, at night a singles scene. Durkin's sponsors several teams, so volleyball, baseball, darts, ski club and rugby enthusiasts are regular patrons. The place is clean and friendly, and here you can drink in a room with a bit of bar history.

9:30am-2am, $, 60¢/$1.15, # 9am-9pm, 3 dom/3 imp, pinball/bowling/pool/darts/foosball, fm and juke.

Durty Dick's Pub

5961 W. Grand   237-2777
B. Whelan & T. Clifford, props.

On the corner of Grand Avenue and Austin Boulevard you'll find Durty Dick's, an Irish music bar. You can get Harp, Guinness, John Courage, and listen to Irish rebel ballads and folk music, from Wednesday through Saturday nights. For a music bar, the place is cheap. There's no cover or minimum, beers are 70c, and mixed drinks, doubles, are $1.25. Up to 300 people will pack themselves in here to toss down a few and hear the likes of "The Risin' of the Moon." It's a young, boisterous crowd, and they're apt to sing along with the better known songs.

The decor is pub-like, with large beams and a mixture of English and Irish (as if it didn't matter) prints and artifacts. There are dart boards and the bar sponsors darts tournaments. A good place when you're in the mood for music. In the off hours, it's a pleasant place to drink. When the band takes a break, you can often hear the manager, Tom Hudson, play the bagpipes.

4pm-2am, ¢, 70¢/$1.25 doubles, # M-F 4-8, 1 dom/7 imp, darts + 1, live music Wed-Sun.

The Eagle Public House

5311 S. Blackstone   HY3-1933
Mrs. Casey

Around the corner from a busy 53rd Street, you'll find the Eagle. It's what you would call, even if you hated the word, charming. It's decorated in FDR antique, is comfortable and old. There's a nice curved bar with cheese and crackers laid out, there are a few tables and a nice front window for street watching. Since antiques have become big business, and since bars have been glomming them up by the ton, it's easy to be put off by a "collected" barroom. Most of the things, such as the large round clock, circa late 1940's, have been there for many years. There's a restaurant room on the other half of the place, which has the same venerable feel. There are 30ish murals painted on the walls, some nice mirrors, and the atmosphere is calm. The patrons are a mixed crowd, both young and old, and tend to be the kind of drinkers who sit rather than mill around. If I spent a lot of bar time in Hyde Park, it would be at Jimmy's or the Eagle.

The Earl of Old Town

1615 N. Wells   642-5206
Earl. J. J. Pionke, prop.

This is one of the first Old Town joints, one that survived the 60's and managed to launch quite a few people from obscurity to stardom. Bonnie Koloc is the best example, she's been the house star for years now, and it's a revered Chicago tradition to "go on down to the Earl to hear Bonnie." It's a bare boards funky place with dashes of grunge around the corners. A mess of homemade signs litter the front windows and door, the inside is dark and functional, in that sense of the old folk "club" feeling, where no one is more than 50 feet from the performer, you sit elbow to elbow, and a blue cloud of smoke hangs at the seven foot level.

There's music seven nights a week, open stage on Mondays and Tuesdays, and the cover charge varies with the acts and the different nights. John Prine, Steve Goodman, Bob Gibson and Steve Post are a few of the names that have come out of the Earl, and I'm sure more are to come. During the summer, Earl has a habit of selling hotdogs from a cart in front of his place, he's the aging beatnik with long hair and a vendor's cap and apron. Second City performers, students and staff often wander in, and director Del Close is known for his regular habit of avoiding the music. As the musicians walk in, Close gets to his feet and, resentful that his neighborhood tavern is being transformed into a lowly nightclub, booms out "Well, it's time to go! The musicians are here." He and his friends then stride out of the place.

Mon-Fri 4pm-4am, \$, \$1.00/\$1.75, Sat & Sun noon-4am, # opening till 9pm, 4 dom, live folk music, sandwiches.

Elsewhere

3170 N. Clark   929-8000
Janis, Gilmore, West & Fisher

Elsewhere began as a young people's music dive on Lincoln Avenue. One move later (over to Clark Street) it has undergone a transformation of appearance, if not policy. The new place inherited remnants of interior design from the previous management, who ran a gay disco, so you'll find a few artifacts strange for a Chicago blues bar. Best are the massive mirrors which flank the stage at angles and cast the band into eery dimensions.

Here you can find some of the oldest living Chicago blues musicians still playing. People like Sunnyland Slim, Jimmy Walker, Homesick James, Eddie Taylor, John Wrencher and Erwin Helfer perform at Elsewhere, and some of them are over 70 years old. Patrons are mostly young white fans of the blues.

4-2am, \$, cover varies, 65¢/\$1.10, # 4-9 pm, small wine list, 8 dom/7 imp, game room, blues 7 nights plus Sat/Sun matinees, pizza, sandwiches, etc.

The Embers

67 E. Walton   944-1105

There's another, larger Embers on Walton, off Rush Street. But this one has more seating, lighting, and a piano bar. It's an old timer among Chicago piano bars, and it adheres to the classical form. The room seats maybe 20 people, it's done in red, the piano player trills along, a giggler will sing along out of key, the bartender is in a tux. It's a lively place with an over 40's crowd and an easygoing way. Across the street, you'll find the Magic Pan restaurant with a tiny, copper covered bar that I've always liked. It seats no more than half a dozen people, and it's primarily a service bar, but no one will ever find you there, and they always seem to have civilized bartenders.

5pm-2am, music at 8.

The Embers

1034 N. Dearborn   MO4-1458
Mr. Kilpatrick, prop.

There are ten tables in the room and five stools at the bar, yet three men in tuxedos are there to serve you. It's an incredible room, deeply dark, with white imitation leather booths and white linens shining out. They serve a famous steak menu, specializing in prime rib filets.

For drinking, the bar offers quiet, solitude and retreat from the hurly-burly of the street. I don't think anyone much uses the bar, but if you're in a mood for a tranquil place to soothe the jangled nerves, try it.

5pm-10 or 11 pm, $$, $2/$1.50, no #, 17 wines, $5-18.

Erik the Red

11050 S. Spaulding   779-3033
Donald Marion & Richard Lindstrom, props.

To enter Erik the Red you walk a narrow corridor of chic little shops, then as you step in, space-flight disorientation hits you. The place is huge, lit with illusive color and mirrored so that you aren't quite sure where one room begins and another ends. This beverage emporium may be the largest drinking hall in the city, but the visual barrage of stained glass, Tiffany lamps and collected artifacts makes it difficult to pin down the real dimensions. I know I've seen smaller high school gymnasiums.

The bar is a whole Viking boat, and the dragon on the prow has just the right touch of kitsch—blinking red light bulbs for eyes. There are games of all kinds, roomy booths, a dance floor that lights up, disco music, slides, movies and a fireplace. Ringing three sides of this arena of fun is a second floor loft which allow you to sit at tables and gaze on the wild scene below.

Daytime, it's a good spot to bring the family for lunch or dinner. Kids are welcome, and they can bang away at the games or stare boggle-eyed at the action around them. Nights bring in mostly young people from the Southside and suburbs, to dance and carry on. Erik's serves a full menu, with deep-dish pizza, a commodity not easily found that far south in the city.

One afternoon I sat there gazing at the vast beamed ceiling when a middle-aged man was pointed out to me. The stolid fellow sat quietly on the other bow of the Viking ship, sipping beer with friends. "See that guy?" I was told, "This place used to be his auto body shop."

11:30-2, $, 60¢/$1, # 2:30-6, 2 dom/0 imp, pinball, foosball, bowling, disco music.

Eugene's

lobby level, Churchill Hotel
1225 N. State Pkwy.   944-1445
Gene Sage, prop.

Eugene's is a posh nineteenth century Damon Run-
yonesque place where exceedingly rich people, young
business folk and the indescribable odds and ends of the
Gold Coast hang out. It's a dining room with a mixed
menu, where free hors d'oeuvres, antiques, what nots,
fine cabinets and a full-sized statue of a horse are to be
found. Easy-listening popular music wafts through the
air, the well dressed staff float about, and everything is
elegant and dandy. The cocktail hour, 5 til 7pm, is
popular, but be advised not to enter in your bib coveralls
and straw hat.

5pm-2am, $$, $1.25/$1.75, # 5-7, 300 wines $6-$375, 2
dom/1 imp.

944-1383

Across the lobby from Eugene's is Mon Petit, a French
restaurant. It has a small, nine stool bar and two cocktail
tables. There's a tuxedoed French provincial flair here,
the bar can be intimate. There's a piano player enter-
taining the dining room which the bar overlooks, and
hors d'oeuvres are served from 6-8. It's what is known as,
especially late at night, a classy "sneak" joint.

The Fat Black Pussycat

3019 N. Broadway
Bob Buter, prop.

The Pussycat is a slammo tambourine boogie bar, one of
the original New Town places to drink. Its patrons are
young people who like a blaring juke box. They pour out
the back door into the yard, they sit on the front porch,
they fill two rooms inside.

The building is a crumbling turn-of-the-century house
converted some 25 years ago to a saloon operation. The
bar itself sits in what was probably the living room and a

second (dining?) room is open. The walls are plastered with junko paste-up pictures and there's a well-worn, beat-in feel to the place. The people who come here want a good time, and they're out to get it.

During warm weather, Bob Buter, resident tavernkeeper, throws free barbecues for his patrons. You'll find him leading the pack in drinking, laughing and carrying on. He claims the building is haunted and that he meets the ghost in the hallways now and then. His bar is a lively place and he likes it that way. His comment on this book was simple. "Just don't pass that thing out in the Continental Plaza."

Don't so there if you have zippa trouble.

noon-2, $, 65¢/$1.25, # 12-7, 1 dom/1 imp, pinball, juke.

Figaro's

7 E. Oak St.   944-0685
Charles Gleffe, Robert Morrison, props.

If your are cruising the Rush Street area and suddenly feel like getting away from the deluge of bright white lights, flashing neon and fast club action, stroll into Figaro's. The yellow awning only says "Fig's" on each side, but that's because it extends a mere 18 inches from the building over the front windows, keeping size in perspective. Most people's living rooms are bigger than Figaro's. It measures about 25 by 25 feet, and that includes bar and all. But it's nationally known as an odd, cosmopolitan hide-away. Here you can find famous personalities and performers avoiding the glitter of the lounge scene. Near North residents and the occasional crazy or two drink here, too. Figaro's has been at 7 East Oak for over 27 years, but it suffered a fire recently and has been renovated, so it's changed a little from the way it was in years past.

Noon-4am, c for the area, 75¢/$1, no #, 1 dom/2 imp, no games, mixed juke.

Finley's

17 W. Elm (south of Elm off the alley named Finley
Court)   664-8452
Greg Bush, prop.

This is a recent addition to the seemingly infinite number
of watering holes in the Rush Street area, and it's a
pleasant one. It mixes elegance and comfort and has a
desirable alley way entrance which reminds me of
Neary's Pub off Grafton Street in Dublin.

Finley's was a coach house years ago. Now they have
two bars and a small, enclosed dance floor. The decor is
mostly dark wood, and the bar top is a fine piece of work-
manship. There are antiques, stained glass, mirrors, and
the usual expensive accoutrements necessary for a well-
dressed bar in that area, and it was all put together by
Chicago's latest bar designer, Phil Rowe, It has his look.
There's a second floor where they have, mercifully,
contained the games. Hors d'ouevres are served from 3-8
pm.

Finley's is still young and developing. Perhaps that's
why I like it, the crowd hasn't found it yet.

2pm-4am, $, 75¢/$1.25, # 3-8, 2 dom/2 imp, games,
taped music.

Flannagan's Pub

2939 N. Broadway   348-8744
Rondal Flannagan, prop.

Flannagan's is a crazy New Town neighborhood bar.
People pile in, the juke box is always blaring, drunken-
ness and wild laughter abound, and spilling beer on
your companions is an acceptable activity. This is not the
place to go for a quiet conversation. The crowd is
mid-20's through 30's, and there seems to be a good
number of them who stroll between Flannagan's and the
next crazy pit-stop down the street, Fat Black Pussycat.

The bar is designed simply in dark wood, with a
counter and a few tables. The front windows provide an
important people-watching arena for the Broadway

stroll, which never stops, and as often as not, Flannagan's patrons are spilling out onto the sidewalk.

For all its boisterousness, the place is friendly and has
a definite neighborhood quality. Saturday and Sunday
afternoons are good times if you're in a mood to start
early, and you'll probably see Flannagan himself there,
leading the pack with yells and laughter.

noon-2, ¢, 65¢/$1.00, 4 dom/3 imp, pinball, loud rock
juke.

Frere Jacques

1825 N. Clark   787-3255
Jacques Grelley, prop.

Frere Jacques is another saloon that is primarily a
restaurant, but it has a bar that is useful to the average
citizen. There's a nice country French menu that is
sensibly limited and reasonable, and the environment is
as crisp and clean as the red and white checked tablecloths. The bar is small, but the center of the front room
has a seating area that faces a fireplace, a nice thing to
have in Chicago winters. The large front windows face
Lincoln Park, and you sit across from the farm in the
park. Grelley has an interesting collection of racing car
steering wheels displayed on the walls, and he was a
professional driver himself. He's competed in the Grand
Prix, Le Mans, and the Monaco races, and his steering
wheels are displayed along with others, including
wooden pre-1915 wheels. There are also rare racing
posters and a track full of toy-sized racing cars. This
aspect of the decor isn't overbearing, however, and it's a
comfortable place for a drink. And, by the way, it's very
popular on Bastille Day.

11:30am-3pm & 5:30pm-10:30pm, $, $1.00/$1.50, # 5-9,
French wines, 2 dom/1 imp, French cabaret music.

Gaffer's

2873 N. Broadway   525-2560
M. Scriba, B. Geraghty, & T. Casey, props.

Gaffer's is a place where incredible crowds of young
people pile in to revel. They literally swing from the
rafters. You'll find boisterous folks throwing coasters and
popcorn in the air, dancing and generally doing a year-
round New Years Eve party.

The music is oldies rock tunes played by a dj
Wednesday through Saturday. There are sock hops on
Thursday nights, and monthly costume contests. The
room is big and uncluttered, there's sawdust on the floor,
framed prints on the walls and a small game area tucked
in one corner. The bar sponsors innumerable teams (8
volleyball teams, for example) and organizes trips and
picnics. Maybe that's the secret of Gaffer's success. Or
maybe it's a 60 cent beer and that old rock and roll
music.

3pm-2am (Sat & Sun 1pm-2), ¢, 60¢/$1.00, # 4-7 M-F, 1
dom/1 imp, pinball & electronic, juke and oldies rock.

Gaslight Corner

2858 N. Halsted   348-2288
Steve Madjar, prop.

The Gaslight Corner is simply a good neighborhood
tavern. The bar is plain with white stucco walls, stained
glass, hardwood floor, nothing terribly fancy. There's a
small liquor store in an adjacent room where you can
buy a bottle from a good wine selection and drink it at
the bar. There's a home-style kitchen serving sandwiches and German bratwurst plates. In the basement,
Mr. Madjar has a huge Rathskellar with booths, a fireplace and a small bar. This room is for rent for private
parties.

The Gaslight is right across the street from the St.
Nicholas Theatre, so there are theatre goers and performers found mingling with the neighborhood crowd.

The place is comfortable, cheap, and offers a good selection of wines and beers. The bartenders wear white aprons.

10am-2am, ¢, 50¢/75¢, no #, 8 wines at bar, 12 dom/8 imp, pinball, juke.

Gaspar's

3159 N. Southport   871-6680
Dean, George & Pete Karabatsos

At the corner of Belmont and Southport, which is a little out of the beaten track, you'll find Gaspar's, a jazz club.

Back in 1900, when breweries used to build taverns the way oil companies build gas stations today, Schlitz built this place and much of the original design has been preserved. The bar room has undergone some changes over the years, but it is light, airy and clean, with a healthy amount of hardwood.

The back room, where the music is performed, is still intact. After months of stripping off paint and linoleum, the Karabatsos family has restored a hall, complete with stage, where your grandmother's wedding reception may well have been held. It's been many things over the years, from dance hall to political meeting place, and now it welcomes jazz musicians. Acts vary, and the cover/minimum charges vary with the group.

11am-2am, $, # 4-6, 8 wines, 4 dom/5 imp, no games, jazz 7 nights, medium-sized menu.

Gavin's

47th & Winchester

This is the Southside's version of the Oxford Pub. That means that it's the place where everyone goes when the 2 o'clock places close. Especially on the weekends, you'll find the drinkers in their 20's and 30's pouring into Gavin's for cocktails till dawn.

The place is simple, darkly lit, and it has a good selection on the juke box, which puts out a clear sound. There are pinball games and a nice large fish tank at the front wall. Gavin's is popular, as are most 4 o'clock places, for what it has to offer, namely a place to go with everyone else when you're thrown out of your favorite tavern.

$.

Gay Women's Bars

For the most part, gay women who run bars have wished to be kept out of this book. Their preference is for a social privacy not invaded by tourists and gawkers. If you are a gay woman unfamiliar with Chicago's gay scene, get a copy of either "Gay Life" or "Gay Chicago News," which are free circulation newspapers. They have social directories and entertainment listings, and are found in most gay businesses.

Geja's

340 W. Armitage   281-9101
John Davis, prop.

The bar has room for only 10 places, but they can be 10 of the best seats in town. Geja's is an elegant cheese, wine and fondue restaurant, and you might be one of the lucky 10 people at the bar. If not, try the comfortable outdoor terrace in warm weather.

The bar is cosy, it has a nice tiled top, the glassware gleams, free cheese and crackers are available, candles flicker. Across the room Tomas, Chicago's best known professional flamenco guitarist, performs. He has become a Chicago legend, performing for Geja's for 13 years, since their original opening on Wells Street.

The restaurant is in a courtyard half a level down, set in a landmark building which is over 80 years old and a healthy example of 1890's Chicago architecture.

Geja's is a wine lover's paradise. One of John Davis's techniques is to invest in wine. He works with buyers in

New York and Europe who gather lesser known, excellent wines for storage. Currently he has 5,000 cases of wine tucked away, and he prices them for the customer based on his cost at the time of purchase, not on the current market value. The list is always being revised, but you can expect to find between 100 and 200 selections priced from $4.50 to $15. Try Geja's when you're feeling intimate, elegant and thirsty.

5pm-11:00 (Fri 12:30, Sat 1), $, $1.25/$1.50, wine list, 0 dom/2 imp, Tomas playing flamenco Fri, Sat & Sun, classical guitarists on the other days.

Germania Inn

1540 N. Clark   MI2-9394
Karl Roessner, prop.

The Inn is on the Clark Street side of the landmark Germania Club building, built in 1888. The bar is nice-sized, not too small, though the place is primarily a restaurant. Old dark wood panelling, bartender in a white shirt and tie, sombre stained glass, red-checked tablecloths on the tables behind you make this a comfortable retreat from Sandburg Villageland outside the door. There's a moderate-sized German menu with sandwiches, steaks, chops, daily specials, German sausages, and, of course, strudel. You can eat anything from the menu at the bar.

    The Germania is a pleasant and subdued spot for the drinker. If you're near-north, at Lincoln Park or Old Town, it's a walk away. The quiet, neighborhood quality is relaxing, the prices are reasonable and the service is friendly. German beers and wines are available in abundance including great weissbier. Closed on Sundays and holidays.

Noon-midnight, $, 50¢/$1.25, no #, 25 wines from $3-10, 12 dom/6 imp, no games, unobtrusive musak.

The Ginger Man

3740 N. Clark   549-2050
Dan Schmitta, prop.

The Ginger Man is a snug, tucked-away bar that en-
compasses several social groups. It's run by a group of
non-bar people. "This is strictly an amateur operation,"
the bartender told me "we make no pretense to professional status." That's okay with me, but he wouldn't say
yes or no to my question whether or not the bar was
named after Donleavy's novel. I guess that information is
too erudite for us common folks.

The Ginger Man is oddly designed with doors on two
sides, brick walls, lots of windows, mirrors and a pot
belly stove. The patrons are from the neighborhood or
theatre goers from the Victory Gardens next door.
Wrigley Field provides some fans who spill in after
games, and the Near North hip crowd is beginning to
identify the place as a find.

As it is, it's a comfortable little place for a drink and
conversation. There are a few extra wines and a nice
selection of beers. The only complaint: a few tasteless
tits-and-ass prints on the wall, which the bartender
eagerly pointed out to me (as an asset) as I left.

Mon-Fri 3pm-2am, Sat & Sun 1pm & 2pm, $, 50¢/$1, 5
dom/18 imp, pinball, juke.

Glenshesk Public House

4102 N. Kedzie   267-1755
Jim McCallan, prop.

At Glenshesk you'll find live Irish music, a lot of
drinking and some dancing. The bar top and table tops
are bright green. The usual Irish stuff adorns the walls,
and after a busy first year McCallan expanded the place
to double its original size. The Irish whiskey bottles are
hung upside with those mechanical shot pourers they
use in Ireland. On Sunday evening at 9:30, the Irish
hour is broadcast on WOPA am from Glenshesk, with
live music and announcements affecting the Irish com-

munity. The musical groups vary, though they're always Irish, and performances are on Wednesday through Sunday nights. You'll find two rooms, both large and rambling, and a mixed crowd of people of all ages. Sandwiches are served and there's a $1 cover on weekends. The place gets jammed, especially when there are sing-alongs and a foot stomping good time to be had.

Mon-Fri 4pm-2am, Sat & Sun noon-closing, $, 90¢/$1.25, # 4-9, 6 dom/3 imp, pinball, live Irish music.

The Gold Coast

501 N. Clark   329-0565
Larry Seewald, mgr.

This is Chicago's gay, sado-masochistic, chains, leather, motorcycle, Western levi bar. If that surprises you, then you should know that the Gold Coast is not only known around the world, but it advertises around the world, in motorcycle journals and other leather bars with its collected posters, calendars and t-shirts. It is the home bar of one Etienne, who paints the half-naked muscle-bound idols in various suggestive stances and adorned with the appropriate leather and metal accoutrements. There's a set of his murals on the walls in the bar, and his poster series is tacked up around the place.

The bar is, appropriately, a bare boards joint, with no attempts at prettifying or frilling. The leather men stand about, drinking beer from cans while the juke pumps out tunes. It's the kind of place that has reserved Thursday nights for the different Chicago motorcycle clubs. It's a strange world for the outsider.

The Gold Coast has been in business for 16 years, and this is its fourth location. Full length feature films are shown on Sundays, and Tuesday night is Leather Night, with discounted prices on the drinks.

4pm-4am, $, 75¢-90¢, 3 dom, pinball, pool, juke.

The Golden Ox

1578 N. Clybourn   664-0780
Fred Sinn, prop.

The Golden Ox has been an important German restaurant since 1921, when it was one of the many of its kind in a traditionally German neighborhood. The neighborhood fell on its face a few years back, taking with it the much lamented Sieben's Brewery and beer hall. Now, much like the Como Inn about a mile south, the Ox is an unusual island in a deteriorated locale, but it doesn't matter once you're inside.

The bar itself is of handcarved golden oak, and it serves as a display for a mass of German collectibles including ceramic steins, hand carved statues that are also whistles, cuckoo clocks, and innumerable other items. The barroom is small with several stools and four tables, it's a regulars place with lots of banter and laughter, and it can trick you into believing that you're in the Rhineland. Fred Sinn has a serious wine cellar in the basement, three German beers served in liter or half liter steins, and if you order a glass of white wine you get a split of a very good Deidesheimer Kabinett.

This is a landmark restaurant with a comfortable and friendly bar, complete with cheese and crackers laid out and zither music on Friday and Saturday night. Overhead, as you drink, there is suspended a statue of a woman with no legs. She is a sort of patron saint of German drinkers, representing an actual woman who lost her legs bringing brandy to the front line soldiers during WWI.

11:00-closing varies, $, $1.00/$1.75, # 11-6, 50 wines $6-$35, 1 dom/3 imp, zither on weekends.

Golden Shell

10063 S. Avenue N   221-9876
Maria Peloza, prop.

Chicago has an East Side. Not everyone knows it, and some deny it, but it exists and there are thousands of citizens who live there, who call it that, and who should know where they live. The Golden Shall is in the East Side, and it's the neighborhood's original Yugoslavian, immigrant, longshoreman and steelworkers bar. The East Side is an economic fiefdom of U.S. Steel, and just about everyone who comes in the Golden Shell is somehow connected with that inconceivably huge corporation.

There's a long, old bar, lots of stools, rows of tables, and a $2.50 plate dinner that will fill you up. Lots of men in working clothes and stocking caps line up here to toss a few down. The place is staffed by a team of Yugoslavian women who tend bar, waitress, and hostess the rear dining room. Now, the rear dining room is a surprise. It's Eastern European elegant, with tablecloths, candles and a lady in a full length dress who will seat you. There's another bar in this huge room, and there's occasionally entertainment.

Across the street from the Golden Shell is a dock yard, replete with ships and cranes, and this sets the mood for the neighborhood. The Shell looks like a dump from the outside, inside it's a pastiche of funky immigrant decor, mixed with American carryout and classic tavern. If it weren't such a long haul from the rest of the city, I'm sure that in a short time it would be a "find", the menu would change, prices would go up, they'd redecorate it and it would be ruined. As it is, it is alien, not quite comfortable for the outsider, and priceless, but cheap.

¢.

Jim Gorman's

22 W. Elm   337-1252
Jim Gorman, prop.

Any tourist who's been in Chicago for more than 24 hours knows that the Rush Street area has its perils. Not that you'll be killed by gangsters or shanghaied on an ore barge to Gary. It's simply a matter of spending too much money and not having a good enough time. There are the strip joints, gay joints, the old traditionals, the hideaways, the music joints, and the singles scene. Where to go?

In the competitive arena of the singles saloon industry, there's been a San Francisco design boom over the last several years. Plants, antiques, brass, stained glass, hardwood all combine to assault your eyes in these places.

In this morass of Rush Street singles bars, a fellow named Jim Gorman has had the nerve to open a place that has a simple design. You walk in and your eyes snap in shock. There's *no* 1880's English wrought iron trellis-work holding carousel horses and bust of Plato and stained glass china cabinets with dead plants. There's none of that. The place is simple. It looks nice, people go there to talk and drink. They have real plants. I can't say any more, except, go to Gorman's.

4pm-2am, $, 75c/$1.25, # 4-8, 2 dom/limp, no games, taped music and juke box.

The Great Gritzbe's

21 E. Chestnut (enter from State St.)   642-3460
Lettuce Entertain You, Inc., prop.

Lettuce Entertain You Inc. owns most of the flashy saloons with the funny names in Chicago. One thing they've always been aware of in their restaurants is the value of having a large and comfortable waiting area, should the dining room fill up. If people can lounge about and drink while they wait for a table, everyone's happy. At Gritzbe's they've done their best in creating a lounging room. It's designed by Tony Barone and it's as big as most bars. The room is half filled with a ramped, sculpted seating gizmo that has steps that serve as seats and tables. Here you can plop on the small mountain of grey carpeted environmental furniture and drink.

They offer a free cheese bar for drinkers, which is one of the tastiest and most generous offers you'll find in Chicago. Chunks of cheese, cheese dips, crackers and raw vegetables are laid out for the taking. There are a number of colorful house drinks, those soda-style creations with fruit, served in bowl-like glasses, and a few interesting specials. They have pitchers of Bloody Marys or martinis served with a tray of vegetables and dip that is a bargain at $3.95, and the wine list is acceptable.

Gritzbe's is a popular after work place for the well dressed young professionals who prefer a fashionable environment, and the free cheese makes it a great place for the hungry drinker.

11:30-midnight, $, 85¢/$1.50, # 3-6, 11 wines $4-$8.50, 2 dom/3 imp, electronic table games, tapes.

The Greenhouse

12th Floor of the Ritz Carlton Hotel
160 E. Pearson   266-1000
Marban Corp., prop.

On the site of the old Pearson Hotel stands the Ritz-Carlton, its lobby is on the twelfth floor. On one side of the floor you'll find the Greenhouse. Now we've all seen the boom in plants and greenery in drinking spots, but the Greenhouse takes the prize. Where other places have plants, here we find trees. Set on a brown and white mosaic floor, there are wicker couches and chairs, glass top tables, plants, flowers, a forest of green. The glass ceiling slants up to meet the rest of the building. Acres of windows let in the light and an electric powered canopy runs down should the overhead glare be too much. Looking out over the lobby, you'll see flowers, a large fountain with an excellent sculpture sitting in it, and murals high on the walls. There are bamboo lamps and woven wicker wall coverings.

There's the quiet come-and-go atmosphere of a hotel lobby, with plenty of room, over 120 seats. Cheese sticks from the Ritz C. pastry kitchen are served, and you can select from over 300 wines ($7-$200). Try this place when you have an uncontrollable urge to sit on the veranda of your equatorial villa, but don't have time to go there.

11am-1am, $, $1.50/$2, wine list, 1 dom/2 imp, no music.

Grover's Oyster Bar

2256 W. Irving Park   588-4662
Bob Arp, prop.

The bartender stretches over the bar to serve a bottle of wine to customers. He explains that the headwaiter, Paul Sweeney (wearing blue jeans and a flannel shirt) will get grouchy if he has to work too hard. The "soon to be famous" Grover's is a seafood restaurant with the manners of a real tavern. It's a nice combination. They have one fishnet that dangles over the bar in token gesture to nautical decor, and the rest is cornball tavern.

You can get good seafood here, from gumbo to lobster, and they have a nice, inexpensive wine list to wash it down. The menu is a la carte and includes oysters, clams, froglegs, pike and crab. You can eat at the bar, elbow to elbow with the neighborhood working people. You can eat lobster in painter's coveralls. It's a combination that appeals to someone like me, who invariably fails every dress code devised by man. Give it a try. Closed on Monday.

Tues-Fri 11:30-11:30, Sat & Sun later, ¢, 65¢/$1.00, 20 wines $4-$10, 8 dom/8 imp, juke.

Hamilton's

6343 N. Broadway   HO5-9240
Richard M. Doan, prop.

Hamilton's is incredibly unattractive from the outside. A monstrous neon sigh which doesn't work gives the place the air of an old movie palace. The face of the building is grimy black and a collection of signs done in faded, greasy-grill lettering announce the best cheeseburgers in town. The door looks like it belonged to a speakeasy.

But don't be put off. You can't judge a bar by its . . . Inside, the place is a fantastic funk bar where workingmen, college kids and neighborhood everybodies come to drink. There's a college bar feel about it (Loyola University is just up the street) and pinball, foosball and pool are found in the back room. Large photos are hung over the booths, showing cityscape scenes of Chicago in the 1930's.

The original owner was L. Hamilton, who opened Hamilton's in 1932. Mister Doan took over the place in '37 and his two sons, James and Tom, work the place for him now. The Doans live above the bar, and the place is a fine example of the Chicago family tavern. Give it a visit if you're nearby.

Hamilton's is on a strip with a slew of bars, all vying for the Loyola/Mundelein business. Shazam's, across the street, is good for weekend disco dancing, if you do that. Minstrel's and Huey's, a block north, are rock and roll hell holes, Broadway Joe's, a wholesome place, is to the south, as is the Pumping Company. To the west on Devon Avenue is Cunneens, the infamous citadel of semi-sleaze, the Unameit, and the city-famous Irish immigrant bar, Connelley's. If you throw a brick in this neighborhood, the odds are 3 to 1 you'll hit a tavern.

10:30-2, ¢, 60¢/85¢, 4 dom/0 imp, games, good juke.

The Hange Uppe

14 W. Elm St.   337-0561
O. McKinney & P. Rezilio, props.

The Hange Uppe is representative of the Rush Street young people's disco-madness movement. On weekends, they pile into the two-level self-billed "distinctive discotheque," creating a wall-to-wall mob scene. Holding a drink can be an accomplishment. There's one bar upstairs, with a d.j. and dance floor. Downstairs there are two more bars, another dance floor and a game room. The design of the place is pleasant enough, but if you go there in the peak hours it doesn't matter since the scenery is young people dancing, dancing away. Early in the evening, backgammon is popular. Dress is casual. Drinks are reasonably priced.

Mon-Fri 5pm-4am, Sat & Sun 5pm-4am, $, 60¢/$1.25, # til 9pm, 3 dom/0imp, backgammon, pinball, disco.

Harry's Cafe

1035 N. Rush St.   266-0167
Harry's Cafe Inc.

Harry's Cafe is the latest addition to the Rush Street area.
In Chicago there are two nouveau-hip conglomerates
that are leading the dining and drinking business.
There's the Lettuce Entertain You group (Fritz That's It,
Lawrence of Oregano, Jonathan Livingston Seafood, R.
R. J. Grunt's, The Pump Room, and the Great Gritzbe's)
who specialize in an active, nearly-entertaining food
service with a young, hip staff and a striking decor. The
designer, in this corner, is Tony Barone, who isn't afraid
to use sculptural and color effects on interior environments.

In the other corner we have the Harry's Cafe Inc.
people (Shennanigan's, Mother's, River Shannon, Clark
Street Cafe, Harry's Cafe). Their design champion is
Phil Rowe. His handicap is that, while Barone uses color
and flexible materials, Rowe prefers to work in wood.
Now I like the wooden-antique-brass-stained glass look
that has swept Chicago. It started in San Francisco in the
"fern bar" of the late 60's and is in many ways an admirable and elegant design for the drinker. My complaint
with Rowe, and with Harry's Cafe, is that it's moved
towards the direction that Holiday Inn has taken. When
you're in a Phil Rowe place, by God, you know it. While
drunk, you might easily forget which one. Somehow ex-
quisite antiques and fine craftsmanship with hard wood
become stereotyped. Now if you enter only one or two of
the places, it's hard not to be charmed, but the seasoned
traveler and battle-weary drinker easily picks up the
pattern and becomes a bit bored and irritated with it.
There is a danger in any fashion becoming fixed, and I,
for one, would like to see a more inventive and inno-
vative movement in bar design.

As it is, Harry's is beautiful. It's full of plants and elegant Rowe *objets,* and as a Rush Street single's haven, it
can do no wrong. Everything is tasteful and comfortable, from the matches on the bar to the potpourri menu,
which offers a generous selection of tasty food. There are
two bars and three rooms, lots of glass windows, where

you can gaze from your table and bentwood chairs to watch the passersby in the street. The patrons are young, well dressed, and there's a 50 per cent restaurant feeling to the place. In a sense, I feel bad that my design criticism falls on Harry's, for it is probably the fullest and most graceful of Rowe's works to date. But it is also the latest, and for that the pattern must be pointed out here.

11am-2am, $$, $1.00/$1.75, # evenings, 16 wines $4.50-$10.50, 3 dom/1 imp, taped music.

Hashikin

2338 N. Clark   935-6474
James Sakata

Imagine a traditional Japanese tea house with ladies in kimonos serving people who are sitting on the floor. Sake, served in the tiny cups, is poured next to Japanese beer. Add a piano, and a piano player who plays only Japanese music. No food is served, this is strictly a cocktail lounge, and it exists on Clark Street, Chicago. For the weak of limb there are also booths.

7pm-2am Mon-Sat, $, $1.50/$1.50, 2 imp, Japanese piano bar, from 9pm.

Hobson's Oyster Bar

448 N. State (side door entrance)   642-1906

Hobson's is reborn. You'll notice when you approach the gleaming brass door to enter. The city's renowned place for dark, dank drinking, gumbo and oysters was closed for five months in 1977. After a change of ownership it underwent a complete interior remodelling. You may remember that old feeling it had, dark as the lower levels of hell, subdued, a bit shabby and plain dirty. No one ever minded, and tons of gumbo were washed down over the years. The new proprietors, who prefer anonymity, cleaned and refurbished the downstairs from top to bottom. The bar, for example, was stripped, then sealed

21 times. The floors are redone and new wooden panelling is on the walls with a touch of polished brass here and there. They're no fools at Hobson's, though, they're keeping the lighting as dim as ever, so you can barely tell that the place is clean, and the dark, intimate, escapist mood is much the same.

Hobson's has been a Chicago tradition for over 40 years, and you will find it jammed at lunchtime, after work, and on weekend nights. There's an upstairs room that's primarily a dining area for the overflow of people, and while it's not as dark as the barroom, it's hardly bright. Next to the barroom is a glass enclosed oyster bar, where a man in white will shell the beasts for you. The place is basically the same as it was in the old days, where dark and privacy were valued. As the proprietor put it, "There's a whole lot of intimacy going on around here."

11:30-midnight, $, 75¢/$1.10, 5 dom/2 imp, juke.

Hogan's

1 W. Erie (corner of State & Erie)   944-6998
Jim Hogan, prop.

Hogan's opened up in what was Joann's, that infamous melting pot of old. Joann has recently opened up a new place, over on Wells Street, in case you missed her. But at Hogan's very little of the old Joann's is left. The place was stripped of that New Orleans bordello funk and redone in wood, tiffany and plants.

Hogan's is small, comfortable and unpretentious. The location is in a type of limbo: off-Michigan Avenue, off-Rush Street, yet not really in a residential area. West Erie could be called a commercial slum. You get a mixed crowd of office and studio workers from the nearby commercial art area. It's a big lunchtime and after work place, and they serve the nationally famous muffaletta sandwich, a poor boy from New Orleans with an olive salad thrown in. They also have Huber's gemulichickeil on tap. It's a naturally brewed all-malt beer without the usual American-favored poisonous additives. Gemulichickeil has to be shipped in refrigerated trucks so it won't spoil, while Schlitz, for example, is chemically inert. A stein of Huber, for 50c, is a grand bargain at Hogan's. Berghoff's and Otto's are the only other places I know of that serve Huber of Monroe, Wisconsin. Hogan's is closed on Sunday.

10am-1am, ¢, 50¢/$1, 2 dom/2 imp, juke.

Hogen's

4560 N. Lincoln   334-9406
Bette & George Hogen

Lincoln Avenue was once an Indian trail, then a thoroughfare north for white settlers. At the turn of the century it was a route to Evanston. We all know about "last stops" before the wilderness. In the 1880's the last Gasthous (inn) before the woods was the bar that is now Hogen's. Inside, you'll find photos from 1900 and 1910 showing a few of the boys knocking back what a sign describes as a K. C. Scmidt pale extra. Another picture has a runaway cart rammed through the front windows of the bar. The frontier of the photos is now the mid-north side of Chicago.

The Hogen family has had the place for some 30 years, and it remains a fine place to go. Half of the room is a restaurant where dirt-cheap German plates are served. Each day of the week a different menu is featured with simple, good food. The bar is panelled, clean, and hearty. Neighborhood drinkers drink here, and the banter can get loud and robust.

To give you an idea of the place's looks and how typical it is of the tavern scene here, the now-defunct TV series *Mama Kovac* used Hogen's as the Kovac family tavern. The prices are good, there are German wines and a good selection of imported beers.

9am-2am, ¢, 50¢/80¢, 8 dom/12 imp, stereo.

The Hotsie Totsie Yacht Club and Bait Shop

8 E. Division   337-9128
Gary DeAngelis, prop.

Gary DeAngelis describes The Hotsie Totsie Yacht Club and Bait Shop as "a neighborhood bar in a night club district." The bar's theme is nautical, with oars, life preservers, block and tackle, and the *piece de resistance,* Chicago's only section of nautically inclined stained glass from an old church on the East Coast. At the Hotsie Totsie you can get pina coladas, strawberry and banana daquiris, made from scratch with fresh fruit, what DeAngelis calls "groovy sandwiches," and a pleasant place to drink. The Yacht Club shows no evidence of being patronized by yachters, and the atmosphere is easier on the nerves than most of the places in the area. DeAngelis, a high-energy saloon keeper, dashes up and down the bar swapping lies, telling tales, cracking jokes, razzing customers and ringing a ship's bell which hangs above the bar, when he finds something particularly noteworthy or hilarious. The bar itself is double-sided, giving DeAngelis an opportunity to get closer to the action instead of being separated from it.

So, when you're undecided about what you want, maybe what you need is a fresh banana daquiri, a groovy sandwich and a Yacht Club full of people but no sailors.

11am-4am, $, 85¢/$1.25, 4 dom/1 imp, no games, juke.

House of Tiki/ Cornell Restaurant

1612 E. 53rd/1610 E. 53rd
Tiki Ted, Julian Krum, props.

They sit side by side on 53rd Street in Hyde Park. They both have large neon signs proclaiming their existence.

Both are restaurants with bars, and both are open until 4 in the morning. That's their advantage, since most places in Hyde Park close at 2, it's convenient if you're in the neighborhood to have two 4 o'clock joints side by side. If one depresses you, as 4 o'clock bars can so easily, you need only walk a few steps to try the other.

The Tiki is a Polynesian restaurant, and the bar has that usual bamboo-rope stuff that never fools anybody into thinking they're in Polynesia. After 2 in the morning the Tiki can slide into a state of sophisticated semi-sleaze that you can only find in Hyde Park. Ladies and gentlemen of the night line up to talk, drink and wait till 4.

The Cornell is an old-timers restaurant with a small curved bar. Things are '40-ish here, with a sense of faded elegance. The bar is padded, quieter, and by its looks you would probably expect it to close at 10 rather than at dawn. Neither of these places are outstanding, though both can be useful and comfortable for the late night, Hyde Park drunk.

Tiki: 11:00am-4am   Cornell: 11:30am-4am

Ile de France

1177 N. Elston   278-0114
Jacques Pele, prop.

The Ile de France lies in one of Chicago's most preposterous and enchanting locations, the corner of Division and Elston, a block or so east of the Kennedy expressway. This place, formerly Rich's Mariners Inn, sits on the banks of the Chicago River, under the Division Street Bridge. Surrounded by industrial wasteland and flanked by a shipyard, you find a full-blown French restaurant with bar and cocktail room. In the summer, boaters and yachters can tie up at the restaurant's dock and come ashore for a meal or a few quickies. The place, with brilliant white linens in the dining room, a dark, leatherette-cocktail lounge atmosphere at the bar, and a variety of Gallic decor, is literally mad situated where it is.

At the same time, it holds a real attraction. Where else can you get a bottle of French wine, put your feet up, and watch Goose Island (or at least a couple of its warehouses) while the Chicago river splashes by? In the summer there are picnic tables outside, at the water's edge. If you're lucky you can witness an on-water traffic jam when a surplus of the Ile's boaters have docked and a barge can't get by. Since there is no competition, you have great stretches of legal parking space to choose from in front. So, the next time you are engaged in conspiracy, subterfuge or adultery, try the Ile. You can't get further away and still be in the heart of the city.

3pm-2am, $, 75¢/$1.25, no #, full wine list with a French emphasis, Old Style and Kronenburg (French) beers, no games, no music.

Import Tap

10429 S. Ewing   734-9275
Tom Bender

Down on the East Side there are countless taverns in the area where U.S. Steel dominates the scene. The Import Tap is one of the better taverns in that part of town. There's a small bar in front, and a row of padded booths in the back that could have been in a 50's soda fountain. Half of the business here is food, with daily specials, seafood and a slew of sandwiches. You'll find it to be a family place, with kids and couples coming to have a meal after work. The bar is traditional tavern style, with two tv's for the sports events, and a choice of seven draft beers. There's a large selection of carryouts, and the usual snacks and odds and ends to be bought. Four days a week they open at 8am, steel-town style, and there's a regular flow of neighborhood people. You wouldn't travel across town to come here, but it's a good example of a steelworker's bar.

Mon 10-2, Tue-Fri 8-2, Sat 10-3, Sun 12-2, ¢, 30¢/65¢, 4 dom/3 imp, electronic games, FM.

International Cocktail Lounge

O'Hare Airport   International Building
Carson International, prop.

If you have time to kill at O'Hare Airport, this lounge is often the most interesting place to while it away. Directly across from Swissair and Scandinavian air lines is this haven for the world traveler. It's basically a simple bar, with three physical attractions. The first is the bank of windows which gives you a closer view of the airplanes than you'll find anywhere else at O'Hare. The jets park and roll away right outside. Then there's the massive wall hanging, a sort of rug nouveau sculpture which is generally ignored while it collects dust. The highlight for the discerning cosmopolitan eye is a glass-enclosed wall of bottles. Bottles, the object of millions of hours of hard staring for the reflective drinker. These bottles are encased, they are half gallons, and they are upside down, rigged with tubing to the computo-mechanical booze-pourer behind the bar. You order gin, the bartender presses a button and, bless the modern age, you can see bubbles rising in the gin bottle across the room as your alloted portion flows into the glass.

But the real event here is the parade of people. Any race, nationality, language or costume is a normal event. Maybe you can sit next to an ambassador, a spy or a smuggler. Depending on the flight scheduling, the predominant nationality of the patrons can be Spanish, and half an hour later Eastern European. The peak hours are from 3-7pm, though it's also filled at other odd hours. The bartenders and waitress are often bilingual, they currently speak German, Spanish, French, and Arabic, although, as I was told, "a whole lot of pointing goes on."

10am-11pm, $, 90¢ (15oz)/$1.35, 3 dom/2 imp.

The Irish Village

6215 W. Diversey   237-7555
James O'Neill

The Village is the elegant Irish supper club of Chicago.
It's clean, well organized and modern, designed in that
mock style you'll only find in America, which says: this is
what it would be like in a "real" tavern. There's a thatch
roof over the bar, prints and paintings of the Irish countryside, the crests of the provinces, and the American
flag. The only touch missing is a picture of John F.
Kennedy, though local politics are rather well described
by a huge mural of the posting of the Irish Declaration of
Independence on the front of the Dublin Post Office in
1916. Mr. O'Neill is from Galway and almost all of his
employees are from Ireland. The room is large, with rows
of tables which are used for dining from 5pm-9pm. Then
it's just drinking accompanied by live Irish music. Reservations are a must on weekends, and you'll find all kinds
of people here. There are pints of Guinness and Harp
and an Irish coffee with whipped cream. Tuesday nights
are popular, with corned beef and cabbage as the
special, and on St. Patrick's day the place is, of course,
insane. There's a corny leprechaun's corner with tiny
tables and stools, and there's not a bad seat in the house
for watching the musicians. Closed on Monday.

11am-2am, $, 80¢/$1, # 11-5, 5 wines at $8, 3 dom/5
imp, live Irish music.

Jasper's

2554 N. Halsted   549-2520
Lee Stanley, prop.

Jasper's is a newcomer to the near North singles bar
scene. The interior is new-style Chicago-young peoples-
bar, with brick walls, antiques, hardwood, stucco and
dead (chemically treated) plants. There's a fireplace,
and a surprisingly large and comfortable beer garden.
They offer every possible draw on drinks to get the
masses in. There are 2 ladies nights, a t-shirt night,

Sunday is half-price day, et cetera, et cetera. Sandwiches are served. No one knows who Jasper is.

11am-4am, $, 60¢/$1.00, # 4-7 and Sunday and other nights, 6 dom/6 imp, pinball/bowling, juke.

Jimmy's *aka*
The Woodlawn Tap

1172 E. 55th St.   MI3-5516
Jimmy Wilson, prop.

Chicago Magazine is so fond of the place that they've put it in their "In The Clubs" listing, which is pretty funny when you think about it. Jimmy's is the University of Chicago's sprawling, venerable tavern. The design is Early American Bar, using furniture that you could dance on, functional in the manner of folding chairs. Jimmy has had the place since 1948, and it looks like he took up the place and abandoned ideas of ever redecorating on the same day. It's a landmark bar, a Hyde Park tradition that deserves respect the way too few places in the city do. The first room is the original barroom, and it's weathered and beaten in by the many thousands of drinkers who have passed through here. Jimmy's added on another storefront with two small rooms. The front one is nice, it has streetside windows and a small service window that lets you deal with the front bar without a lot of walking. The "University Room" is still another storefront, complete with its own bar and a variety of collectibles hung on the walls. This room is also comfortable and has its own identity, separate from the others. Years ago the University Room was reserved for University of Chicago students, but since that's illegal the practice was abandoned.

Since Jimmy's provides a funky environment that welcomes the neighborhood as well as the students, you'll see barroom arguments erupting over philosophical questions as well as who won the pennant way

back when. Students, writers, workers, and the usual
Hyde Park stew of citizens fill the place. You should too.

10am-2, ¢, 55¢/75¢, 15 dom/20 imp, no games, ancient
tv, FM, sandwiches.

Joann

730 N. Wells   337-9010
Louis Jacobone

Joann's is back. After nine years on State Street (where
Hogan's is now) the place closed down for two years and
reopened in the autumn of 1977. The new place sur-
passes the old in that shameless, brazen, New Orleans
bordello design which is utterly admirable, a sense of
taste not seen elsewhere. If Chicago has a decadent
Parisian-style cafe scene, it's found at Joann's. The place
is frequented by a strong mixture of artists and lawyers.
This is what Joann inherited from the area surrounding
the old place. There's also a fine mixture of washouts,
decadents, young office people, laborers, aging hippies
and musicians. There's red and black flecked wallpaper,
a tintype ceiling, tables with mismatched chairs, a
gaudily colored jigsaw-puzzle carpet, statuary, mirrors
and muted red and yellow lighting. There are photos of
Joann herself, her mother and two sisters, her aunt and
uncle and Louis' ex-wife. You'll find the lovely Joann,
one of Chicago's grande dames of salooning, holding
court here with her wild mixture of friends and ac-
quaintances while Louis handles the piano at Chicago's
rowdiest and most unpredictable piano bar. Literally
anyone may wind up playing the piano, singing or
singing alone. Some great musicians will show up, and
anybody's drunken sister may be belting out tunes at full
voice. Louis has thousands of old songs memorized, and
he amazed me once by playing "East of the Sun, West of
the Moon," which I had requested. Go to Joann's. It's set
up anew in what was an antique store then a massage

parlor, and though they say they're not yet finished with the decorating, it's a wonderful place.

4pm-4am, closed Sundays & holidays, $, 75¢/$1.25, 1 dom/0 imp, pinball, free peanuts.

Joe Danno's Bucket O'Suds

3123 N. Cicero   283-9485
Joe Danno, prop.

It is a proud tradition among Chicago tavernkeepers to be crazier than the next guy. Harlan and Bob from Sterch's pose for a Reader ad in wedding gown and tux. Steve of Cunneen's says "What do you think this is, a fag bar?" when you order something as fancy as a whiskey sour. They drink like crazy or not at all. They spend fortunes on outlandish dinners, drinking bouts and mega-tips. There's not a drinker without a crazy bar owner story. Of them all, I decree, with due respect, Joe Danno to be the craziest.

He has this little tavern on Cicero which serves pizza and other foods. It's old, worn and beat in. He is a booze expert. There're over 800 bottles behind the bar, including ancient brandies, pre-Prohibition bourbons, Danno-made liqueurs and things you or I have never heard of. He'll tell you the difference between Cognac and Armagnac. He'll have you taste strange, strange liquids. He'll explain how every damn thing is made, where it's from and how old it is. It is reasonable to say that if you get talking with him about his boozes, and if you start sampling, you will leave woozey, if not drunk.

The walls are covered with a million or so labels from what has come and gone here, and at the rear of the place is a room-sized cooler box from the Pleistocene era. Go to Joe's. It is one of Chicago's mad landmarks. You can stare at the back bar forever, it's an endless altar to imbibing. The rear of the lower bar opens to the kitchen where several members of the family are usually hanging out. It's funky, grungy, incredible. The whole place could be crated, shipped to the Louvre, and displayed as a masterpiece of surreal art.

Hours can be irregular.

John Barleycorn

658 W. Belden (Lincoln & Belden)   348-8899
Eric Van Gelder, prop.

The Barleycorn is a long-time Chicago favorite for low-key drinking and hamburger dining. It's a subdued, dark, and quiet atmosphere with a large collection of hand built miniature ships displayed on shelves. Classical music is always the music of the day. There are slides of paintings flashed on screens on the walls and a collection of parlor-room paintings is to be found.

Old-time silent movies are run more-or-less continuously, so you can watch Laurel and Hardy or Fatty Arbuckle at the Barleycorn while munching and sipping.

Many Chicagoans have fond memories of the Barleycorn as being one of the first of the Bohemian bars. It has been known for its music, its comparatively intellectual environment, and for its absence of the usual blaring bar noise and glaring bar junk. Over the years, however, it's really failed to develop a barside culture, and the emphasis has settled on dining at the tables. Often, when you enter, you'll find it easiest to get a seat at the bar, which can be just what you want. Let them eat burgers.

11:30-2am, $, 70¢/$1.10, no #, 7 dom/10 imp, no games, classical music.

Kelly's Pub

949 W. Webster   LI9-9150
Clover Corp., prop.

When the writers for the dining and entertainment sections of Chicago's newspapers are looking for a real, salt of the earth tavern to profile in the weekend paper, Kelly's Pub is a perfect example of what they'll pick. It opens at 7am! And, old men and women sit next to college kids and office people on their way home from work! Kelly's sits under the el and they watch ball games on tv.

Kelly's has all the qualities to make it a funky find if you are from Long Island, say, and are unfamiliar with Chicago's taverns. In my social continuum of drinking from dives to elegance, it ranks middle road. It's a nice neighborhood tavern with 2 or 3 different crowds a day. There's the 7am til afternoon hard core, the dinner hour working people, and the nighttime DePaul student young folk.

Bears and Notre Dame football games play an important part in bar life here and it's a good place for just sitting. Kelly's motto is, "You're a stranger here but once."

·7am-2am, ¢, 50¢/80¢, 6 dom/3 imp, pinball, bowling, juke.

Mr. Kiley's

1125 W. Belmont   549-8524
Frank Kiley

Mr. Kiley's used to be a real redneck country and western bar a couple of years ago, until an ever-growing invasion of the Near North young people took it over and made it a place that now advertises in the Reader. The old customers, those with bouffant hairdos and cowboy hats, moved on down the street to the Skyline, a country-western bar that still looks like it belongs in Kentucky. At Kiley's you'll find a blue-jeaned more-than-casual scene with one of the few places you can dance without undergoing the dress code scrutiny. There are many things about the place I don't like. The air is always dingy and smokey, the drinks are generally lousy, the beers are limited to canned Schlitz and Old Style and draught Old Style. The wine will give you a belly ache, and it ain't cheap either. But there's no cover or minimum and the music is good. The Sidemen with Janice Horst have been playing there for quite awhile, and they do a good job of young people's country music. They're not the same as the old timers with the twang in their voices, but they do well with a dash of rock and roll in their performance. A good number of professional dancers from Chicago companies like to come here to unwind, and it's one of the Near North's only 4 o'clock dance halls. Mr. Kiley's has a "country kitchen" with passable food served until closing. The action doesn't really start here till after midnight, and Tuesdays are open mike nights.

7am-4am, Mondays til 9pm, $$, $1/$1.50, 3 dom/0 imp, pinball, live music 6 nights.

King Arthur's Pub

126 S. Wells   346-6797
Arthur Lieberman, prop.

If you're downtown and in the mood for a tankard of Bass ale, drop into King Arthur's. Decorated in antiques and British artifacts, you'll find a dark pub-like atmosphere.

There's a pub room, where drinks and sandwiches are served, a saloon and a full dining room. Back in the dining room there's a piano bar where customers traditionally sing old favorite tunes.

Good as a change from the usual loop scene.

11am-11pm, 5 days a week, $, 75¢/$1.25, no #, extensive wine list $$, 2 dom/2 imp, no games, piped-in music.

Knight's Inn

2612 W. 69th St.   476-0299
Paul Sakalauskas, prop.

In a short three blocks on 69th Street there are eleven taverns. Most of them are small neighborhood Lithuanian bars such as the Club Gintras. If you're in the mood for an ethnic bar crawl you can spend an evening here. The notable Tulpe restaurant is in the middle of this section, at 2447 W. 69th, and it's recommended high for home-style Lithuanian food. The Tulpe opens at 8am and serves until 8pm, so you could dine early and hit the streets for drinks. But you could walk up and down 69th a dozen times and still miss the Knight's Inn.

There is no hint, from its exterior, that anything of interest lies within, even the windows are curtained. The address, 2612, is your only clue. Open the door and you walk into what could be the cocktail lounge of a ski resort in Colorado. It is a modern, lodge design with brick walls, cosy tables with candles and a fireplace. It's a dark quiet retreat used mostly by couples who want a place where conversation is possible. It's spacious, intimate, comfortable and a certain surprise, considering the location. It used to be a bank.

There's a back room, also dark and low key, and you'll find chess, scrabble, backgammon and a pong table. The work of local artists is displayed on one wall, and the paintings I saw recently were excellent. The Knight's Inn is most popular in winter, when the fireplace is roaring and the illusion of being in the mountains is strongest.

If you look like a Black, a hippie or a communist, the other small taverns on this street may not welcome you. In fact, if you don't speak Lithuanian you may be as welcome as a spider on a wedding cake. Some of the places have those bogus "Members Only" signs to keep strays out. The Knight's Inn, however, is the cosmopolitan center of Marquette Park.

5:30-2 (closed Monday), ¢, 60c/80c, 2 dom/0 imp, stereo.

La Bello Sorrento

9485 S. Ewing
M. Loprino, R. Koch & A. DeMarco, props.

"It's a glorified neighborhood bar," says Mark Luprino of his place, and it's true. Under the shadow of U.S. Steel on South Ewing, Sorrento's offers a comfortable place to drink for those in the area who don't want to go to "Mom's", "Ed's Tap", or the countless other Ma and Pa joints on the ethnic East Side.

Sorrento's is panelled, with curtained windows and a lounge-like decor. There's a well-stocked bar, good Italian food (10% discount if you eat at the bar), and a friendly atmosphere. The area's professionals tend to gravitate here, and they've established a tradition of trivia banter, even to the depths of "name the colors, in order, of the original roll of Life Savers." It's an after work place, popular on weekends, and the bar has a life of its own, separate from that of the restaurant, an important point for the drinker.

11-2, ¢, 50¢/75¢, 18 wines $4.50-$7, 7 dom/2 imp.

La Concha

2745 W. North Ave.   486-9309

La Concha is a Puerto Rican night club, patronized primarily by young members of the Humboldt Park area. It's an adventuresome expedition for outsiders to brave the neighborhood, but La Concha is certainly an interesting cultural tour. The place is a Benny Goodman era ballroom with orchestras of over 15 musicians each. Dancing is why most go to La Concha, and the dance is the Salsa. The Salsa is a sexy reverse mambo with a few flourishes thrown in. The music is a Caribbean 4-beat and the dancers spin, pause, gyrate and spin again in a hypnotic choreography that's wonderful to watch. There are one or two orchestras per night, and they can really pound out the beat. The women are generally formally dressed, in a variety of gowns and dresses, and the men are natty as well. Dance here, even if you have to fake the Salsa stuff. Between sets the floor is hit with disco stuff that pales after the Salsa. The bands come from New York and Puerto Rico, so there's a varying cover charge that can go over $4. Open only on weekends and holidays.

9pm-2am, Fri, Sat, Sun only, $$, $1.50/$1.50.

La Mere Vipere

2132 N. Halsted   549-9120
Tom Wroblewzki, prop.

La Mere Vipere was a gay neon-palace disco that couldn't make it on Halsted Street, so it opened its doors to welcome everyone and became the punk rock headquarters of the city. Chicago's Warholesque scenes are decidedly tamer than New York's, and in that sense you'll find La Mere to be more entertaining than frightening. It's a two-story dance bar with neon flamingos, a wall-shaking sound system, strobe light, et cetera.

There's no dress code, all types of people are welcome, and you can dance to the neuron-smashing beat of punk rock.

People lead each other around on leashes, wear plastic bags, entangle themselves in fish line, glue rubber spiders to their faces and do all those fashion things we love so well. On weekends, especially when they hold the punk fashion show, you can observe all the multi-sexual levels of Chicago interacting in costumed splendor.

La Mere will no doubt ride the wave of fashion and popularity, so when punk rock is subsiding this place will pick up on what's next.

Wednesday's drinks are 2 for 1. There are special events and occasionally parties for popular musical groups, such as the Ramones.

8pm-2am, $, 85¢/$1.10, no #, 6 dom/0 imp, pinball, punk rock.

Lawry's Steak House

100 E. Ontario   787-5000
Lawry, Inc., prop.

Surprise. Lawry's (the salad dressing) steak house has a little-used bar and lounge that's one of the best of its kind, which is the turn of the century English gentlemen's drawing-room-stuffed-furniture salon. Here the bartender wears a crisp white bandleader's coat, the furniture is comfortable, with a generous number of couches and lamps. Prints, clocks, chandeliers, floral carpeting and a metal bartop fill in the decor.

In 1890 the building was one of the McCormick mansions, later it was the Kungsholm puppet playhouse. The second floor has one banquet room remodelled by

Lawry's, but the third and fourth floors are still in their original design. Now there's the restaurant and the bar, which is a little-known sleeper in that part of town. When the dinner hour rush is not on, you'll find only a few folks scattered here and there in two large rooms. There's an "attitude adjustment hour" from 3 til 9 Mon-Fri with hors d'oeuvres and a piano player. The place is quite beautiful, in its way, and certainly worth your investigation.

Mon-Thurs 11:30 am-11:00pm, Sat 4:30-12, Sun 3-10, $$, $1/$1.65, # 5-9, 58 wines, 3 dom/2 imp, taped music.

Leo's Southport Lanes

3325 N. Southport   DI8-9277
Leo Beitz, prop.

Leo's is terrific. It's the city's last-of-a-dying-breed. A bar with its own adjacent 4-lane bowling alley, they have real live pin boys. Kids hop about behind the scenes, risking their limbs to reset the pins for you. Bring your family and all the children you know, stand behind the bowlers and watch with awe as they work. "See," you can say, "there are real people back there, they are called pin boys." Get to Leo's before the powers decide it's a nice spot for a hi-rise.

Leo's is a sturdy Chicago building done in "olde English" pub design, both inside and out. In the bar room there are dark beams, leaded stained glass, a marble floor and serious hardwood everywhere. The bar has interesting wooden barrels with shing steel hoops set into its lower frame. "Everyone like them until they bang their knees," the bartender explains. The booths are dark, deepset and attractive, only the quiet thunder of the pins gives you the hint that through an archway lie the bowling lanes.

The bowling room also has a pool table, lockers, ball racks, pinball, and seating. You'll find yourself walking about in silent reverence, finding that here, in this place, a bowling ball polishing machine can be beautiful.

I'm told Leo's is the oldest place of its kind in the city, and the second oldest in the country. It was built in 1945, so there's a comment on how fast we've been tearing things down to build things up. Outside there's a fresh sign that reads "BOWLERS WANTED," and inside the bartender, a friendly lady with a smile, told me bravely "We need pinboys." Go there.

M-F, 3pm-2am, Sat & Sun noon-2, ¢, 45¢/75¢, no #, 5 dom/no imp, bowling, pool, pinball, juke box.

Lindy's

3689 S. Archer Ave.   927-7807
Mr. Linderman, prop.

3865 South Archer Avenue is an oddball building, sort of a stretched rectangle, and when you walk in there's the bar, its stools, and room for only one person to pass before the wall stops movement. The name of the game at Lindy's is chili. They have a good, basic, barely-seasoned bowl of chili served with oyster crackers. You order a drink and a bowl, the bartender turns to one of two windows cut in the back bar and yells, "Bowl!" to the kitchen and you get it in seconds. Hot stuff is provided for those who like it, but Lindy's chili is set for the common denominator of American taste.

Lindy's has been there since 1922, when it started as a hotdog stand. Now it's one of those architectural oddities that you find on Chicago's slanted streets. Its exterior is plastered with Coney Island style billboard print describing the sensual delights of the chili, and it gives you the feeling that you're in one of those diners converted from a railroad car that still thrive in the East. There are games at one end, a green linoleum bartop and ordinary working people at the bar. All in all, it's a grand place, the center of the city. The menu also has burgers and things, but it describes the carry-out chili this way:

bowl $1.00
pint $1.70
quart $3.20

half gallon $6.00
gallon $11.40
In the great American tradition, the cook is Oriental.

10am-midnight, 10-1am weekends, ¢, 80¢/85¢, 4 dom/
1 imp, pinball, electronic, juke.

The Lion Bar

909 N. Michigan   Lobby level, Continental Plaza
Continental Plaza Hotel, prop.   943-7200

The Lion is decorated in the manner of a large library,
with couches, wing backed chairs, lamp lighting, carpeting, and real books on shelves around the walls. The
bartenders wear those hotel jackets and bow ties, the
waitresses wear red waistcoats and, seemingly, stock-
ings. It's a place where you go to wait out the storm, your
fatigue, the rush hour, or whatever else the big city
happens to rain on you. It's a retreat. The atmosphere is
transient, due to the hotel travelers coming and going,
but a good number of Chicagoans use it as a place to toss
down a few. They serve massive doubles from 11am til
7pm, and there are munchies on the tables. After 6 you
can get sauteed mushroom caps for a dollar and scampi
for two. The management describes it as a "fiercely attractive retreat," (Lion, get it?) and it looks like some of
the better hotel bars you find in Canada or Great Britain.
There's a bar to sit at, complete with tv, and a piano
player entertains from 8:30 til 1am (7:30 Sunday and
Monday). Barring the doubles during the day, it's
expensive, to go with the fiercely attractive decor.

11am-1am (2am Sat), $$, $1.50/$2.25, 10 wines $6-$15,
11am-7pm, 8 dom/2 imp, piano bar 7 nights.

Little Joe's

1041 W. Taylor St.   829-5888
The Assenato Family, props.

A dozen or so years ago hard times struck Little Joe's,
when the University of Illinois smashed away half of the
Taylor Street neighborhood in order to build the
Chicago Circle Campus. In the process, Joe, sitting on
the edge of the destruction, lost many of his neighborhood patrons to urban relocation. In time, however, the
new University community merged with the old neighborhood, the barriers softened, and now, happily, Joe
has the best of two worlds.

College students have learned to blend with the Taylor
Street menagerie and Little Joe's is still a neighborhood
bar where the locals come in for a drink.

Thirty years ago, when Joe Assenato Sr. opened his
bar, Taylor Street was the first, central Italian section of
the city. It won't do you any good to look up and down
the street for gangsters, but yes, the neighborhood has
that kind of history. The bar is small and cosy and good
Italian food is prepared personally by Mrs. Assenato.
Lasagne, mostaccioli, manicotti, and antipastos are
created by her hands. Her sons work the bar, and
nieces, nephews and cousins hang around treating the
place like a living room. Since family has gone out of
style in the last decade, it's nice to see a few generations
of the same family under one roof. Probably, you'll find a
young Assenato at a table in the rear, doing his (ugh)
homework. Everyone may not agree, but in a world of
lounge plastique, a kid doing his homework in a bar is
reassuring and even heroic.

This neighborhood also has the Vernon Park Tap, at
1073 West Vernon Park Place. This bar is the much less
integrated, authentic Italian tavern. There's a bare
boards interior where you can get good food and cheap
drinks. Strangers are less welcome here than at Little
Joe's, though the adventurer can find it to be an exciting,
often boisterous place to tour.

11am-11pm, $, 60¢/$1.00, wines & chianti, 4 dom/3
imp, juke, food served 11:30am-2:30pm and 5:30-8pm
only.

The Lobby Bar

163 E. Walton   751-8100 ext. 286
Playboy Clubs, prop.

Years ago it was the Knickerbocker Hotel bar, during WWII it was an officers' club, and now it's the lobby bar of the Playboy Hotel. You'll get your drink in a super-large stemmed glass with a Playboy swizzle stick, and you can sit and watch the lobby people pass by. The bar was once in an enclosed room, but now it's open and the traffic flow of the lobby streams through. There are couches and cafe tables, a 6 by 6 foot television screen, the room is carpeted and large windows view Walton Street to the north.

In the evenings there's live music and the regulars, travelers, business men, and stewardesses drink the drink of the rabbit.

M-F 11am-1, Sat 11-2, Sun 12-1, $, $1.50/$1.50, 1 dom/1 imp, table electronic games, live music Tues-Sun 6:30-12:30.

Lutz's Continental Pastries and Cafe

2456 W. Montrose   478-7785
Lutz's, prop.

Lutz's is a German bakery which specializes in those elaborate and dainty pastries which are as full of calories as they are of taste. Behind the bakery there's a cafe, and beyond that there's an elegant outdoor garden, used in warm weather. There's a small menu which offers vienna coffee, coffee cake, cookies, ice cream creations with or without liqueurs, soups, a cold buffet and, of course, whip cream tortes or your choice of petits fours. Lutz's has a predominantly German wine list, and half a dozen beers and liqueurs.

Here you can sit in a room as comfortable as some-one's dining room at home, with a carpeted floor, cur-tained windows, and bustling waitresses in black dresses and crisp white aprons. Eastern European elegance is impressive and the glassware, cups, and silver service are thoroughly convincing in their attention to detail. The garden is a cozy place to sit, it gives you the feeling of a countryside inn.

Sundays, you'll find it crowded, and there may be a wait for seating. Lutz's is a neat solution if, for example, you want a drink and a friend wants coffee and a pastry. One of the nicer advantages is that you can stop off in the shop on the way out and get a quadruple layer chocolate torte or two to go.

Cafe: 11am-10pm, $, 90¢/$1.25, 28 wines $5.25-$8, 1 dom/5 imp.

Marge's

1758 N. Sedgewick   944-8775
Marge Landeck, prop.

During the last years of Prohibition, they made gin in the bathtub on the second floor of Marge's and sold it across the bar downstairs. Marge's has been a tavern for over 70 years. It's a near North neighborhood tavern with a typical air of funk. There are wood floors, white stucco walls, that ever-present mushroom-cellar bar aura, and a comfortable mixture of young and old patrons. It's been Marge's place for 22 years, and it's the kind of corner tavern that's never full and never empty. The half pound hamburgers are renowned in the city. They are still hand pressed rather than pre-formed, and they are generous and juicy.

On Monday nights, Al Gray, an underworld Chicago nightlife celebrity, plays ragtime piano. This man is ancient, Black, and blind, and he's a wonder to hear.

noon-2am, $, 60¢/$1.00, 3 dom/4 imp, pool table, pinball, electronic, juke.

Marina City Ship's Bar

300 N. State, lower level, Marina City
Romas Corp., prop.

I hate nautical decoration. Seafood restaurants are the
worst, with clam shells, netting and starfish dangling in
your face. I would rather eat lobster in a French pro-
vincial than a nautical place, and that's saying a lot.

The bar at this place is shaped, of course, like a ship,
with the appropriate brass fittings, fish nets, and
belaying pins. It's well done, if you like that kind of
thing, but I suggest that you steer right past the ship and
grab a table on the window side. Floor to ceiling
windows run along one wall and they are right over the
Chicago river.

While I hate nautical design, I greatly enjoy watching
water while drinking. As the old seagreen Chicago River
slushes on by, you should remember that the river is the
reason why Chicago is here in the first place. Back in
Indian times it was used as a link between the Great
Lakes and the Mississippi River system. DuSable, a black
explorer, and the first non-Indian Chicago citizen, built
his cabin on this river and set up a trading operation.
The river used to flow into the lake, fouling Chicago's
water, so in 1900 the river was reversed by means of a
canal to the Des Plaines River so that we now foul other
people's water. If you want to immerse yourself in the
subject, you can bring along a copy of Harry Hanson's
book *The Chicago* and learn as you drink.

Reflect on all this as you sit at Marina City. You can
watch the cityscape, the yachts, the ships when they
come in, and the occasional raising and lowering of the
bridges over the river. If you want to look inside, there's
a sing-along piano performance 7 nights a week, and a
full menu is served for lunch. But for me it's the river.

11am-2am, $, $1.00/$1.25, # 4:30-7, wine list, 6 dom/2
imp.

The Marquis

10008 S. Western   239-9091
Bill Morris, prop.

There are untold eccentric bars in this city, and the Marquis ranks as one of the most pleasantly crazy places around. The Marquis has an interesting history. A classical pianist named Bill Morris studied under Bernhard Weisser and then opened a lounge. He did it at 100th and Western, a real cultural sink, and he put in a 9-foot concert Steinway. Bill got a 4am license for his bar and he started playing his piano all night. He played "only commercial and modern jazz tunes," and you'd think he would've starved to death long ago. But he didn't. It's a miracle, Chicago-style. Of all things, the younger crowd roared in, liking the whole thing, driving the middle-aged patrons away. So Bill's comfortable dark lounge with mirrors and everything done in black filled up. What to do? Get a new Concert Steinway and build a new, multi-level elegant place right down the street at 9936 South Western and call it The Keys. As a final touch, make the place a private key club, lock the doors and hope. Now there are two and everyone's happy, especially Bill who plays at both.

Try the Marquis, it can be fun, and if you're interested inquire about membership in The Keys.

Mon-Fri 4pm-4am, Sat & Sun 1pm-4am, $, $1.00/$1.00, # 4-9:30, 7 dom/1 imp, live piano.

Martingayle's

1820 N. Wells St.   664-4562
John and James Roth, props.

Martingayle's received the first liquor license issued after the Chicago fire. It was here that proprietors of the Park Club, a successful speakeasy during Prohibition, blew away the police captain's bag man during a shakedown. He had grown too greedy to tolerate. During the 50's and 60's it was the notorious Vieux Carre, 4 o'clock den of mad dogs and fist fighters. But now it is a pleasant seafood restaurant.

As you face the building from the front, what appears to be the first floor was once the second; there's another storefront buried under Wells Street, which was once one level lower than it is now. The rear of the restaurant covers four maple bowling alleys that were in use some 100 years ago.

Martingayle's is primarily a restaurant, but I recommend it as a bar as well. You can eat from the menu at the bar, except on weekend nights, and there's an excellent oyster bar serving blue points, cherrystone clams, shrimp and crab cocktail, creole gumbo, clam chowder, cold crab, cold lobster, mussels and a variety of seasonal dishes. Better than beer nuts for the hungry drinker.

The barroom is dark and comfortable, pleasantly designed, and you're in a building that's housed taverns for over 100 years.

11-2am, $, 75¢/$1.25, 35 wines, 1 dom/2 imp, pinball, juke & FM.

Melvin's

1116 N. State   664-8356
Melvin's Inc., prop.

What Melvin's is known for is outdoor eating and drinking and people-watching. Here you can sit and watch the Rush Street area human parade stroll by while you guzzle a drink and gobble quiche. Inside there's a dining room and a small bar, but tradition has it that you sit outside.

The attraction, of course, is the people. You'll see everyone from lost sailors to the old black man who sings old tunes while he accompanies himself with harmonica and the beat of a lard can. There's a piano player after 8pm, and wonder of wonders, the place opens at the crack of dawn, 7am. Finally, the matchbooks claim that it's "Melvin's Truck Stop."

7am-2am, ¢, 60¢/75¢, 3 dom/0 imp, no games, juke & piano.

Meson del Lago

158 E. Ontario   649-9215
Bill Contos, prop.

You've heard of salad bars, but have you been to the world's only taco bar? For $4.95, the Meson del Lago offers an incredible do-it-yourself taco buffet. Tortillas, tostados, enchiladas, eggs, rice, beans, gaucamole, cheese, sour cream, sauces, and quarter pieces of chicken are laid out in splendid array. It amounts to a 3 course meal at any other restaurant.

Here you can heap your plate high with Mexican goodies, sit in the bar, order Mexican beer or pitchers of Margueritas and please the palate. The design is traditional Mexican: white stucco, terra cotta floors with tile inlays, arched windows, and wrought iron in the windows that overlook the dining room.

At lunch, and from 6pm til closing, the bar features guitarists playing Mexican music, and appetizers are served from 5-7pm. The wines are Mexican and Spanish, and the Sangria is homemade, as it should be. House drinks using fresh coconut milk and ice cream are available.

One of the most surprising aspects of the Meson is the washrooms. Beautiful Mexican tiles, called asulevos, cover the counters and each sink is cast in the same tiled designs. Brass fittings for the sinks were repeatedly stolen, so less dramatic substitutes are in their place. But piles of fresh linen towels are available. I've never been so impressed with a john. If washrooms count in ranking the city's best restaurants and bars, Meson wins first place, seats down!

Meson del Lago, cocina Mexicana, is very pleasant, very Mexican, and worth a visit.

11:30-1am, $, $1.25/$1.50, wine list $5.75-$15, 1 dom/ 2 imp, Mexican music.

Michel's

4648 N. Lincoln Ave.
Peter Michel, prop.

Mr. Michel is an 82-year-old Swiss who owns this place. He has been ill lately, and his employees were reluctant to speak for him, so I don't have particular data about his bar, such as hours and prices. But I can recommend it as a decent bar, the likes of which are dying too fast these days. The place is simple, with little decor at all. You might see it in a 30's movie as a workingman's bar, tables and chairs in the back room, with a clock as the major focus of attention.

The bar is dark, wooden, and again the essence of simplicity. There's a beautiful arched stained glass window over a door on the side wall, plants in the front window and stools at the bar. When he's well, Mr. Michel is behind the bar, in a white shirt and apron, serving drinks to neighborhood people. There's no entertainment, no frills, but you get that quiet and dignified sense of order and propriety that the old, classical tavern can give you.

Mickey's

2316 N. Clark   248-0595
Richard Ropele

Designed in archetypical Chicago tavern, Mickey's is a Near North favorite for those who want their drinks with no frills. Half of the place is a liquor store, there are beer cases here and there, a large TV, team pennants and one of the most impressive collections of snack food I've seen in a tavern. The patrons are locals, all types from laborers to bankers, and their most common interest is sports.

There's a small back room hidden away with a pool table, and this too is cluttered with cases and bar room junk. The total effect is one of Chicago-style warmth and comfort. While the place can be rowdy, it has a very peaceful history, and strangers are welcome. In the tradition of the tavern, Mickey's opens in the morning and carries every known brand of American beer.

9am-2am, ¢, 45¢/70¢, 29 dom/12 imp, pool table, no music.

The Midget Club

4016 W. 63rd St.
Parnell St. Aubin, prop.

The Midget Club is the only bar in the book that I do not recommend, but it's necessary to make a comment on it because everyone expects me to. When folks heard about this book, they'd ask me "Have you been to the Midget bar?" None of them had ever been there, except a few mad bartenders who will travel anywhere for a new place to drink. But everyone has heard of it. I think that most people have a vision of a Barnum and Bailey midgets club, with snappy little people in tuxedoes and gowns, mingling with the occasional standard sized human. Or, they envision a doll's house full of carefully crafted miniature furniture worthy of admiration. It ain't that way. The proprietor is a midget, he was in show business for years, and the bar, tables and chairs are lowered to make it convenient for him. You can pull up a shortened chair to the bar, which is about 3 feet high, and order a beer, which only comes in the "shorties" bottles. That's unusual, and so is watching a midget use two hands to pour vodka in a glass, but after that it's straight downhill. The place is done in hideous linoleum, the kind that isn't afraid to stand up and be bright orange. The drinkers are neighborhood losers, with the occasional sightseer coming to check it out, and there's a depressing glumness in the air. I was there several years ago and came away with that feeling, but the clamor of the drinking populace sent me back recently to check it out. I conclude by saying that no one I've know who's ever been there has recommended it as a place to have a good time, and the only people who are positive about the place have never been there.

Miomir's Serbian Club

2255 W. Lawrence   784-2111
Miomir, prop.

So, you're feeling a little blue and you need a gypsy orchestra to cheer you up? Go to Miomir's. Isaac, a 65-year old Russian, will sing gypsy songs to you accompanied by a five piece band. There's a wailing violin, the crooning of tunes from the world over, and a large square bar where you can sit and enjoy. Miomir's is primarily a supper club that serves an Eastern European menu featuring Serbian dishes. There's kajmak, a fermented milk bread-spread, moussaka, goulash, schnitzel, cevapcici and muckalica.

There's no eating at the bar, and the orchestra is the primary attraction for the drinker. All drinks are $1.50 at the bar, and you can watch the folks come and go. The bartenders are lovely ladies with those Eastern European high cheekbones, and everyone is bilingual. The patrons are often from the suburbs, and they include politicians (mayors and governors, etc.) and other notables. Except for the staff, the place is 99% American, so you'll have a hard time meeting the gypsy of your dreams. Closed Monday and Tuesday.

5pm-2am, $, $1.50/$1.50, 54 wines, 1 dom/2 imp, gypsy orchestra.

The Mirage

731 N. Wells St.   642-2977
Ms. Dianne Banis, prop.

This is what's known as a controversial bar. If you were near Chicago in early 1978, you no doubt heard of the Great Mirage Tavern Pay-Off and Tax Evasion Scandal. As in any Chicago story, there are at least two sides to this phenomenon.

On the side of strict law and order, yes, the Sun Times and the Better Government Association did operate a tavern here for four months and they did provide us with proof of bribe-taking. A fire inspector took $10, a building inspector took $15, and several accountants taught them how to evade paying their fair share of taxes.

The bar denizens of the city generally scoff at the whole event, convinced that given a hundred dollars expense money, any three serious drinkers could form an investigative alky squad that would dig up about 400 times more hard crime by dawn that the Sun Times did in four months. The same group of critics maintain that the reportage was shooting small fish in a barrel, and that the entire event was tainted by the reporters' questionable ratting on their fellow business people and tavern keepers who gave them helpful advice on how to survive in the city. Nailing your neighbors is the lowest crime in the bar world.

The present operation, run by Ms. Banis, is also subject to a running debate. She maintains that she bought and ran the place for seven weeks before learning about the expose. She is, however, an ex-reporter from the *Chicago Today,* and skeptics doubt the probability that a Chicago newspaper person would just happen to buy the media-sensationalistic Mirage just when she did.

Me? I just don't know. What we have is a corner tavern which I checked out before the news scandal, and rejected as being not notable. Nieghborhood working folks and media people hang out there, and the most exciting part of the decor is the back bar, which hails back to the German Pavilion of the Columbian Exposition. The rest is standard tavern. The incomparable Joann's is just across the street.

On the other hand, you can always have a yuk when you go to the Mirage. Pay for your drinks with money stuffed in white envelopes. My kind of town, Chicago is.

10am-2am, closed Sunday, $, 75¢/$1, # Mon & Tues 4-7, 6 dom/1 imp, pinball, juke.

Mister Joe's

741 N. Rush St.
Joe, prop.

"It ain't ivry man that can be a bishop. An it ain't ivry man that can be a saloonkeeper. A saloonkeeper must be sober, he must be honest, he must be clean, an' if he's th' pastor iv a flock iv poor wurrukin'-men he must know about ivrything that's goin' on in th' wurruld or iver went on." These are the words of Mister Dooley, a fictional bartender created in the 1890's by Peter Finley Dunne, a Chicago journalist. Mr. Dooley was a common sense philosopher and Mr. Joe, currently holding court on Rush Street, reminds me of a cross between Mr. Dooley and a stand-up Jewish comedian.

His bar is a working people's tavern in the midst of glitterland, his patrons are the people who work behind the scenes, in kitchens, back rooms and after hours. You'll find maids, cooks, longshoremen and the odd citizen or two stepping down a few steps to enter Mister Joe's. He's got a carry out cooler, half pints, snacks, rolaids, clocks, sunglasses, rolling papers ("flight papers" to Joe), all that junk that's mounted on cardboard, plus Slowik's Delight (horseradish) from Milwaukee Avenue. The bar is small, and well lit, and it's a pleasant relief from the high-powered area surrounding it.

Talk to Mr. Joe. He sits, slugging away cognac, occasionally dozing in his chair, ready for discourse with lively witted people. He'll tell you about God, "The man who turns the other cheek is a fool"; his wife, "She said 'take me someplace I've never been,' so I said, 'How about the kitchen?' "; and himself, "I look like I'm Irish, I drink like I'm Irish, I fight like I'm Irish and I'm crazy like I'm Irish. Maybe Arthur Hailey should check my roots."

Mr. Joe's is worth the trip uptown. Asked when he's open, he replied, "9:30 in the morning until I get drunk."

9:30-?, ¢, 50¢/85¢, 8 dom/2 imp, pinball, juke.

Moody's Pub

5910 N. Broadway   275-2696
John Moody Kahoun, prop.

The exterior design is vaguely cathedral. Arched windows, an austere front and the name Moody may give more than one drinker a spasm of religious association, but don't worry, once you're inside those moments of misgiving disappear. No one will try to give you a tract. In fact, like any self-respecting tavern in Chicago, they kick out the drum-beaters.

Moody's is a 50-50 split between restaurant and bar. Most folks are here to sit at a table and make a burger and beer evening of it. The bar stool action is sparse, and you should bring your own conversation, hustle or fight in the form of friends and companions. A major aspect of the place, much like Otto's on the Near North, is the beer garden. By God, the Chicago Beautiful Committee (and I never knew there was one, nor guessed that they frequented bars) has given the beer garden awards. In the garden, which seats 200, are brick walls, ivy abounding, lots of trees and picnic tables. Birds hop about, there are a couple of not so great fountains, and you have a place to drink away from tavern air. Inside there's a mess of tables, two fireplaces, a TV and a slide projector which shoots the complete Chicago Art Institute slide collection on a screen. That alone can save you a trip downtown.

11:30-2, ¢, 60¢/90¢, 4 dom/0 imp, no juke box.

Moose's Lounge

4553 N. Pulaski   539-0410
Walter Moose, prop.

If you want to hear the likes of "Max Jones and the Southern Sounds," you might go to Moose's on weekend nights. This is a neighborhood tavern with occasional live country and western music and a real moose head over the bar. As a neighborhood place it's quiet, with

streamers on the ceiling, a huge tv screen, free buffet
dinners for the patrons and cheap prices for drinks. The
place goes back to Prohibition, and Mister Moose has
had it for 10 years. The bar and back bar are the
originals. The rear has a stage and extra seating, and a
ceiling covered with hundreds of balloons.

The music is scheduled irregularly, so you should call
to check before you come. A friend described it as one of
the most peaceful country and western bars in the city.
The reason? There's a police station half a block away.

11am-2, ¢, 50¢/70¢, 4 dom/1 imp, pinball, sometimes
live c/w.

Mother's

26 W. Division (downstairs)   337-7006
First Venture's Ltd., prop.

Mother's is the queen of the meat markets. Those who
stroll the Rush Street Area, especially out-of-towners,
usually wind up here, at least once. It's been there for
years, and is one of Chicago's original singles bars.
After 9 in the evening there's live music seven nights a
week, usually blaring rock.

To enter you pass a team of doormen at street level and
go down a long set of stairs to the cave-like bar. There's
usually a cover charge, from 1 to 3 dollars, depending
on the group, but the bar prices aren't bad. There are
two major rooms, the front is a small bar room that
doesn't let you forget that you're in a basement. Here
you'll find the bar, pinball games and such and a sandwich counter. After 9:30 they open the vast, cavernous
back room which has three bars to serve the masses. It's
basically bricks and cement floors here with a few carpeted seating areas. Rumor speaks of remodeling
sometime in 1978. On weekends between one and two
thousand souls will pass through here, with maybe five to
six hundred of them crammed in at one time. There's a
heavy singles scene going on, dancing, drinking and
much hanging around. For sporting events, Mother's

provides a wet-t-shirt-best-tits contest on Wednesday nights.

7pm-4am, ¢, 80¢/$1.30, 2 dom/1 imp, pinball, foosball, live rock, cover charge.

Mrs. O'Leary's Pub

151 E. Wacker   565-1000
Hyatt Regency Hotel, upper level
Hyatt of Chicago, prop.

Not far from the original site of Fort Dearborn, the Hyatt Regency stands, and the Hyatt powers-that-be seem to have taken Chicago history as a motif for their operations. There's Captain Streeter's Cafe, named after the admirable madman who took possession of a landfill peninsula off the lake shore which he called the "Deestrict of Michigan." He seceded from everything currently political and defended his shanty town with several gun battles with the authorities.
  The Hyatt has the Wild Onion night club with live music five nights a week, which is named after the wild onions which gave Chicago its name. Mrs. O'Leary's is a restaurant/bar decorated in antiques and memorabilia, meant to reproduce a turn of the century pub, Chicago style. There's a deli-bar room, the main bar room and a dining room complete with booths that have curtains you can draw for privacy.
  The lunchtime patrons are usually Chicagoans, and at night there's a mixture of local folks and hotel guests. The bar room is a well done reproduction, as befits the coffers of the Hyatt, and is a pleasant hideaway. If the bar is full you can get a drink and sit in a small lobby that overlooks a fountain and a small garden of plants. And, by the way, Mrs. O'Leary's is the title-holder for *Chicago Magazine*'s best cheesecake contest.

11:30-7am, $$, $1.75/$2.00, # 11:30-5, 15 wines $8-$15, 1 dom/0 imp, live entertainment.

Muldoon's Saloon
See Jim Gorman's.

The New Cubby Bear Restaurant and Lounge

1059 W. Addison   525-3210
Thomas Knight and A. J. Vent, props.

Cubby Bear is the massive place across from the front gates of Wrigley Field where, on game days, 6 bartenders work furiously to fill baseball fans with liquids. There are 3 cavernous rooms. One is like a church social hall with folding tables and chairs; then there's the main bar room, and the third is, of all things, a disco room where live entertainment is presented on weekend nights. But the average citizen doesn't go to the N.C.B. Restaurant and Lounge for eating, discoing or lounging. Here's where you go to tank up on game day, for the love of all that's good and American. From the time the doors open at 7am and the fans start to roll in, until game time, when they're pouring out the doors, countless hundreds are lapping 30c draft beers from the same plastic cups they'll get inside the park. *That's* what this place is all about.

The decor is baseball crazy, with pennants and photos of players all over the walls. Among the sports paraphernalia scrap carpeting is nailed here and there on the walls, for no known reason, and there are large coolers stacked with the necessary carry-outs to feed the fans. The N.C.B. is, to describe it by example, one of the few places where you'll find the women's room traffic-controlled with an IN door and an OUT door.

10am-2 (game days 7am-2), ¢, 30¢/80¢, 5 dom/2 imp, 7 pinball, pool, foosball, juke.

The New York Lounge

5151 N. Lincoln   334-8953
Nick Papas, prop.

"Magic! It's fun to be fooled," is the motto of the New York Lounge. All of the bartenders are men and they're all magicians. You sit at the bar, order a drink and the bartender will bring it with a deck of cards, sponge rubber rabbits, pieces of rope and the other traditional paraphernalia of the sleight of hand artist. Cards jump out of the deck, your initial appears magically on the palm of your hand, rabbits multiply, bottles appear out of nowhere. Jack Murray, the place's old timer, still works the bar on weekends, as does Skeets Strum, a magical clown who's worked with Barnum & Bailey and the German Stuttgart Circus.

Nick Papas inherited the place through his uncles, and the tradition of magic has continued for 32 years. During the week two bartenders are on duty, and on weekends the number goes up to five. The performances are directed to the customers individually, so the magic is literally in front of your face, not on a distant stage. The bar is oval shaped. Dark red and black wallpaper and carpeting creates a lounge atmosphere, and there are candles at a number of tables, where a magician/bartender will come to serve/entertain you. The banter of the bartenders is "off color," and is meant to make you laugh while being put a little ill at ease. There's a microphone at the bar that speaks into the women's washroom, for example. But you will be baffled, amazed and amused by the magic.

7am-4am, $, $1.00/$1.25, 2 dom, juke, no cover.

Nick's

1973 N. Halsted   664-7383
Nick Novich, prop.

Nick's, on the corner of Halsted and Armitage, is a newcomer to the near north side. The place was built using old bowling lanes for its tables, a refinished mahogany bar, and a pressed tin ceiling. It has vast windows for street watching, and a huge turn-of-the-century nude hanging over the bar that once was in a museum in Vienna. Sandwiches are served and you can get a weissbier, which is popular here.

You'll find the folks in Nick's to be a mixture of the young blue-jeaned and just about every other type of Chicago drinker.

Rather than being any kind of a "club" that fills this neighborhood, Nick's is built in the fine old tradition of the Chicago tavern, rough hewn.

It's friendly, not overcrowded, and for mysterious reasons known only to Nick, on weekends an authentic itinerant mariachi band strolls in to play at night.

11am-2am, $, 50¢/$1.00, 3 dom/3 imp, pinball, juke & tapes.

The 1944 St. Louis Browns

59 E. Illinois, basement level   644-4338
Bob Roach

This is another in the Chicago series of subterranean bars, but its theme is a bit more unusual than most. In case you're not aware of it, in 1944 the St. Louis Browns won their first and only pennant after 43 years of giving it a go. The team moved in 1954, became the Baltimore Orioles and are living happily ever after. A group of Chicago fans began a club in 1955, dedicated to the glory and memory of their heroes of the past. The club became a bar, and here we are.

You enter by going carefully down a flight of steep stairs and find yourself in a place the size of someone's bar in the basement of a bungalow. In fact, it looks a lot like a bar in the basement of someone's bungalow. The decor is, naturally, 1944 S.L.B.'s memorabilia. Pictures, pennants, newspaper articles, photos (one of the whole team), and all that other stuff is placed reverently on the walls, providing the intellectual stimulation for the place. Pool, pinball and serious drinking are the other major activities. Printers, salesmen and others frequent the place. The lady bartender is often the only woman there, and a rowdy humor pervades. One day, while I was there, Minnie Minoso dropped in. What more can a baseball bar ask for?

7am-4am, ¢, 50¢/85¢, 6 dom/0 imp, pool, pinball, juke.

The North Center Bowl and Pool

4017 N. Lincoln, second floor   549-2360
Guenter & Theresa Kippschull, props.

I recommend this place highly. In an age when the pool room has degenerated to a junkies' hangout or part of a shopping center carnival, the North Center has a classic dignity about it. It is a bonafide old fashioned pool hall with an adjacent bar.

Mr. Kippschull has taken great pains to prevent his place from slipping into disrepute. He has rules. He throws out people who cause trouble. He paints over graffiti. He has even gone to the extreme limit of anti-advertising, for nothing outside his establishment mentions pool. Two Old Style signs, one on Lincoln Avenue and one on Damen, are the landmarks you're looking for. Up a flight of stairs, past the Illinois poly-graph laboratory, and you step back in time. There are 10 massive and ancient Brunswick tables with 900 pounds of slate in each one. The west windows are painted green, there are lamps hanging over each table, and strings of scoring markers hang overhead.

The bar is small and subdued, beyond it there's a game room and then a 12 lane bowling alley with its own small bar.

The clientele is a cultural mix, and the pool room is rarely crowded. The next time you are in formal dress and have the urge to chalk up, go to the North Center. It's the finest drink-serving pool hall in the city.

noon-2, ¢, 40¢/80¢, no #, 7 dom/1 imp, 10 games + pool & bowling, juke & stereo.

Northbranch Saloon

1134 W. Armitage   281-3428
Dave, Jim, Fred & Don, props.

The owners of the Northbranch are all teachers in the
Chicago Public Schools with an interest in carpentry.
They built this place themselves.

Four nights a week there's live music performed,
usually blues or bluegrass, other nights they pull out, of
all things, a ping-pong table. The look of the place is a
cross between a traditional Chicago tavern and the new
design in bars. It's a pleasant mixture.

There's a tv, juke box, and they have cookouts,
sponsor teams and have a lot of the usual tavern
activities. The clientele is young 20's through 30's, and
there's a bit of foot-stomping going on, too.

4pm-2am M-Thurs, noon-2 Sat & Sun, ¢, 60¢/90¢, # 4-6
M-F, 5 dom/6 imp, ping pong, live music 4 nights.

The Old Polonia
aka Warsaw Cafeteria

10 N. Clark   263-0663
Tom & Bill, props.

You walk down a flight of stairs to the basement level,
and you are greeted by a stand containing stacks of
menus. The stand is flanked by a five foot high plastic
orange tree which is, fantastically, covered with about
two bushels of plastic oranges. You are at the portals of
the old Polonia.

The place has a cafeteria counter which runs into a
bar. There are those square tables and sturdy chairs
which this kind of place always has, and red stools at the
bar, which is decorated with red curtains and red floral
print wallpaper. The room is a large, vaulted basement.
People come here to eat simple, plain food and to drink,
all very cheaply. The menu dedicates half its space to
drinks, and the other half to food, each day having a few
specials. Monday, for example, offers corned beef hash

($1.95), stuffed pepper ($1.95) and knockwurst & sauer-kraut ($1.85). Drinks are 85c to $1, and domestic beer is 50c. The place is about as funky as you can get. There's a gallery of photos of the American presidents over the bar, an ancient cash register, and an altar-like arrange-ment of bottles at center bar. All kinds of downtown citizens make their way here, and it's a favorite of an avante garde group of attorneys who enjoy its particular style. A downtown great.

Mon-Fri only, 7am-7pm, ¢, 50¢/85¢, 6 dom/1 imp, no games, tv, juke.

O'Leary's

1157 N. Dearborn   337-7780
Nick Loane, prop.

O'Leary's has been at 1157 N. Dearborn for 10 years. It's the kind of bar that bartenders and waitresses from the surrounding Rush Street scene would frequent, along with locals who prefer something less than total glitter.

The bar is sublevel, dark and quiet. An ancient O'Leary family owned the building years ago, and it's named after them. People play darts here, eat pizza, and talk in the manner of neighborhood bars. You won't find it overcrowded at any time, so there's no rush for the "right" time to be there. At the same time, there's a definite singles scene going on, but one with more calm than most.

Nick Loane, the owner, is a Tiffany glass and lamp expert who hangs his collection in the bar. His last set of glass was so good that some unknown citizens decided to burgle it. In the Chicago "I will" spirit, he's currently working on another.

4pm-4am, $, 75¢/$1.25, # 4-9, 1 dom/4 imp, darts, bowling, juke.

O'Rourke's

319 W. North Ave.   944-1030
Sullivan, Lundberg & Kovar, props.

You've probably heard about O'Rourke's even if you haven't been there. Legend has it as an Irish pub, a writer's hangout and a den of intellectuals. It's also a Near North neighborhood spot without a neighborhood. Situated in limbo between Old Town, a ghetto and Lincoln Park, O'Rourke's must call its patrons from some distance, but the regulars find it acceptable to commute. Huge photos of James Joyce, Brendan Behan, Sean O'Casey and George Bernard Shaw cover one wall. The photos, some Irish posters and Guinness stout are about as Irish as the place gets, however. The back room is the headquarters of some of the best darts-throwing in the city. The bar sponsors national darts competition each year and enthusiasts come thousands of miles to play. I've always found the "writers" aspect of the bar to be over-mysticized. You'll find newspaper men, and an odd author or two, but Chicago's answer to James Joyce isn't to be found lurking behind a pint glass. If you have been to O'Rourke's in the past and found it a bit grubby, give it a second try. Ownership changed hands not long ago and the new proprietors are clean and committed to the improvements that make a bar more efficient. The previous owner was of the grime-equals-atmosphere breed, but now the bartenders are free to wipe the dust and spilled booze away.

Patrons of O'Rourke's are generally of the young, educated, alienated class; not ready for the slick spots or the dives. On St. Patrick's Day they open at 7am and bedlam reigns all day. If you are unfamiliar with this part of the city, park north of North Avenue when approaching O'Rourke's. The crime/danger rate climbs as you go south of the bar.

3:30-2am, $, 60¢/$1.00, # 3:30-8, 3 dom/4 imp, darts, pinball, bowling machine, funky low-key juke box.

Orsi's

1401 N. Wells   787-6604
Mr. Milito and Mr. Orsi, props.

If you should find yourself on Wells Street in the center of Old Town, and you don't like what you see, Orsi's offers refuge. Tucked in with the strip joints, the porn shops, the junk shops and the shoddy glitter of Old Town, Orsi's sits quietly and unobtrusively. It's an Italian restaurant, with an excellent thin crust pizza and a number of veal specialties. The place is done in classic black and red Italian formal design, with flowers on the tables and floral painted globes lighting the room.

Orsi's bar is done in dark wood, there's carpeting, mirrors, and a sense of privacy and quiet. Tuesday through Saturdays there's a piano player, doing corny old tunes. You can eat and the bar and the place is rarely overcrowded. There's a nice sense of old fashioned charm here, and, especially if you are a visitor to Chicago, I offer it as an escape from the Old Town scene.

Mon-Fri 11-2, Sat 4-3, closed Sun, $, 75¢/$1.15, # 5-7
30 wines $5-$8, 6 dom/2 imp, piano bar.

O'Shaughnessy's

6655 N. Clark St.   338-8114
Brian O'Shaughnessy, prop.

In the great tradition of Irish Chicago saloonkeepers, Brian O'Shaughnessy is frothy. When he's not working and drinking in his own bar, you might find him rolling in and out of other places with a pack of buddies, wet shirts, unshaven grins and tolerant women, scattering money and laughter as he goes.

He runs a pleasant Rogers Park place, cozy, not rowdy. It's full of "local folks and North Shore brats," according to him. There's a game room with all the toys you'd need, and a quieter bar room with dark wood, plants in the window and a violin case hung over the bar.

In the violin case is a toy submachine gun and a sign "Respect your bartender."

Lunches are served, from 11:30 til 2:30. 11am-2am, ¢, 60/$1, # 5-8 M-F all day Monday, 4 dom/5 imp, many games, juke box.

Otto's Beer House and Garden Club

2028 N. Halsted   528-2230
Sam Stellatello, prop.

Otto's is a fine example of the beer and burger bar made good. It's gone through several transitions since it opened, and now it's become more of a semi-elegant restaurant than a traditional tavern. There are 2½ dining rooms, the latest being a glass walled greenhouse room with a garden/art gallery interior lit by skylights. But while I recommend it as a place to eat, these are restaurant affairs. For the drinker, the place has whittled down to a small bar, which is primarily a service bar for the diners. The feeling of barroom social life is pretty well drummed out of the place in order to make room for the food.

But in the summer months, Otto's has the best outdoor beer garden in Chicago. Ancient trees loom over tables that can seat 250 thirsty souls. Greenery abounds, and the service is good. Huber's draft is excellent for 55c, and there's a nice selection of 18 wines ranging from $4.75 to $10. The garden is casual, comfortable and a fine place for conversation. So, when the weather is good, which it is occasionally, this is the place to go if you wish to commune with nature Chicago-style.

10am-2am, $, 55¢/$1.25, 18 wines, 2 dom/5 imp, taped music.

Oxford Pub

2263 N. Lincoln Avenue   477-5146
Martin Sinclair, prop.

"Fascination of the abomination" comes to mind when the Oxford is discussed in Chicago bar circles. It's *the* Near North 4 o'clock booby-hatch bar which has few other identifying characteristics. They serve food from 11:30am til 3am, some neighborhood regulars hang out during the daytime, and they sponsor a few teams. But what the Oxford is really about is after 2am, when every semi-drunken fool and his squint-eyed brother take three deep breaths outside and stroll past the rugby-playing doorman, affecting a casual air of sobriety. During the week it can be more or less sane, with a large number of bartenders and waitresses from other joints keeping a near-peace as they line the bar, but on weekends it's zoo-city, putting the Star Wars bar to a pacific shame. It's a big, cavernous place with a funko-orange decor, cement floors and an odor all its own that slaps you as you enter. I confess to a friendly disgust-hate relationship with most of the goings on in the place. On the positive side there's always someone to talk to in the wee hours, and the many barworkers from other places who go there after work keep things amusing and active.

Gird your loins late one Friday or Saturday night and give the Oxford a go. Don't wear anything you wouldn't roll on the floor in, and avoid looking at the nude over the bar, for it's the ugliest objet in the history of conceptual art. Here you can experience Chicago's surreal drinking experience in its finest form. What else could you expect from a place that sponsors the country's only pall bearing contest?

11am-4am, $, 75¢/$1.25, # 4-7, 5 dom/5 imp, pinball and electronic, juke.

Pam's Playhouse

4659 N. Clark   334-2402
Ted Harrison, prop.

Pam's Playhouse is one of the "authentic" country bars
with live music five nights a week. A friend of mine,
Denise DeClue, described it rather neatly in a *Reader*
article: "It's an Uptown, country, redneck bar . . . The
fellas wear cigarettes in their T-shirts, most of the women
come in half sizes, and the Pabst beer, if you want it that
way, comes served in a can."

Bouffant ladies still dance with each other here, and
the music comes with an authentic "twang" in the vocals.
The bar is a rambling affair that splits things so that the
music room is on the far side, and a more brightly lit area
has games and tables for food to be served. Ted Harrison
says of his bar: "We try to have the best in country music
and we cater to the people who don't cause us no
trouble." There's a tradition here that's used at the
Skyline on Belmont and a few other places. If you want
the band to play a particular tune for you, just stick a
dollar on the stretch of tape that hangs from the ceiling
in front of the stage. This act gives your request country
clout.

To give you an idea of the flavor of the Playhouse, let it
be known that it opens at 7am and closes at 4am, and
there's a large sign over the pool table which reads:

POSITIVELY
NO GAMBLING.
by anyone at no time.
Action will be taken.

Yep.

7am-4am, ¢, 50¢/70¢, 6 dom/0 imp, pool & pinball,
live country music Wed-Sun from 9pm.

Papa John's

1157 W. Wrightwood   472-8100
John Wright

This was formerly the Straight Arrow, a place where you

could go to drink and shoot pool without much distraction. Papa John bought it and has cleaned the place up, which is always a dangerous risk for a bar. The drinkers get used to the filth and miss it, but it's still a place where you can shoot pool.

You get pretzels and mustard to munch on, there's a small kitchen, tv, and big open windows to look out. The prices are low. It all adds up to a good, uncomplicated tavern.

10am-2, ¢, 55¢/80¢, 5 dom/2 imp, games, juke.

Park West

322 W. Armitage   929-5959
Dale Riedermaier, prop.

The Park West is the newest show lounge in the city, and it's housed in the remodelled building which used to be the Town Theatre, an old porn palace. The place is very big, with a stark modern design that is simple, semi-plush, and in the Las Vegas style. The seating capacity is 750, and that's at a series of booths and tables in a tiered, amphitheatre arrangement that creates no bad place to sit. There's a balcony which holds the lighting equipment, a second bar, and railing seats up above the rest of the place. The acts, times, and cover charges vary. Bette Midler, Buddy Rich, the Temptations, Bill Quateman, Chuck Mangione and the Glenn Miller Orchestra are a few of the recent acts. When the act encourages dancing, there's a place for it in front of the stage.

The Park West is impressive. Its grey, glass, steel and sculptural design makes it seem an appropriate place to go and spend a bunch of money, while other places give you the impression that you've been had. There's a tuxedoed management and you'll feel more comfortable if you're well dressed. The sound system and acoustics are great. The Park West is also available for private affairs.

Hours vary, cover varies, 2 drink min., $$, $2./$2, 6 wines at $12-$20, 1 imp.

Patrice

914 Ernst Ct.   944-0265
Patrice, prop.

Patrice is one of the new, elegant French restaurants that
finds it more advantageous to advertise by not advertising. We're supposed to find it, or they don't care if we
do, I'm not such which. At any rate, they have a little
hideaway bar where you could meet an agent for a
transfer of documents or jewels.

First of all, Ernst Court is a tiny alleyway (100 East)
which runs between Walton and Delaware, a bottle's
throw from Rush Street. Patrice has one small neon sign
and the windows are curtained. The bar is to the right as
you enter, dark and plush. Here you can hide from the
world in comfort. The back bar is a mirrored light box
that gives you the illusion that the lights run down a
series of square boxes to infinity. Not a kind trick to pull
on someone in his cups, but at Patrice you don't drink,
you have cocktails.

$$

Pippin's Tavern

806 N. Rush St.   787-5435
Tony & David, props.

There are thousands of students at the downtown
campuses of Loyola and Northwestern universities, not to
mention the N.U. medical and nursing students at the
hospital complex near Chicago Avenue and the lake.
Pippin's exists to serve all these young collegiates.
There, on Rush Street of all places, is a college bar. Pin-
ball, foosball, bowling, popcorn on the bar, give the
cluttered look that's a cross between a student union and
a tavern. Pippin's throws a party twice a month and uses
all the usual gimmicks. Sandwiches and pizza are
served.

M-F 11-2, Sat & Sun noon, $, 65¢/$1, # 4:30-8:30,
3 dom/3 imp, games, juke and radio.

Playboy Club of Chicago

919 N. Michigan Ave.   751-8100
Playboy Enterprises, prop.

Here it is, the heart of the international Hefner empire,
home base for thousands of bunnies, the Chicago Playboy Club. In case you thought that it was a thing of the
past, Playboy key sales are still up after 17 years of
business and the young ladies still wear cottontails when
they serve food and drink.

The Playboy Club is located on the first floor of the
Playboy building and is a members-only affair, but if you
are over 21 years of age and alive, you can apply for
membership at the door. The fee is $25.00 for men and
(yes, times have changed) women alike. This allows you
to pass through the gift shop, which stocks all of the
Playboy items that anyone could want, and enter the
"living room," where buffet meals are served. There's
the bar, flanked by a small disco area and by a bumper
pool table where you can challenge the resident Pool
Bunny to a game. The decor makes you feel that you've
walked into a slick, full-page, 4-color magazine
Scotch ad.

Up a curved staircase you'll find the VIP Room, which
is a continental restaurant, a small backgammon corner,
and the Cabaret Room, which offers live entertainment
6 nights a week. Here you can drink, eat, take in the
show, and relax in the center of the empire, where Hugh
Hefner has proved for almost two decades that there's
gold in them thar cottontails.

M-F 11:30-4am, Sat & Sun 5pm-closing, $$, $1.50/$2, 12
wines $7-$14, hors d'oeuvres 6-7pm, 1 dom/1 imp, disco
& live music.

Poor Men's Pub

3149 S. Morgan

The Poor Men's Pub is an archetypical Bridgeport neigh-
borhood tavern. Mayor Daley's home ward is a mixture
of Polish, Italian, Irish and Lithuanian workers who be-

lieve in the American way, the Democratic party, and serious drinking. You can't throw a brick in this area without hitting a tavern. The Poor Men's is across the street from Bev's, down the road from Stan's and dozens of other joints. The place is an average-sized tavern. It's quite clean, with tablecloths on small tables and curtains in the front windows. There's a color tv and the obligatory pool table.

They have their own brand "Poor Men's" vodka and gin to pour for you, there are plenty of half pints, junk food, and a large carry-out cooler. For some reason a collection of ceramic horses is located over the bar. There's a Schlitz globe and the usual beer advertising objects. Mogen David is what you'll get if you order rose, which is a mysterious tradition found everywhere in Bridgeport. The juke box has standard tunes and a selection of ethnic music reflecting the patrons' heritage. This saloon is just the way the neighbors want it, nothing fancy. And, over the juke box, a large Chicago police star is fixed to the wall, the kind you'll find on the side of a squad car. Welcome to Bridgeport, are you registered to vote?

The Portside

3125 W. Montrose   487-7702
Nick, prop.

Here at the Portside, everything is neat, clean and tasteful, and you can eat at the bar and get one of the daily special dinners for $5.95. There are only ten tables, a regulation sized bar, and the usual nautical decor, with paintings of ships, nets and all that seaside junk. The special dinners are served Mondays through Thursdays and they include smelt, trout, lobster, and butterfly shrimp. There is an oyster bar serving clams and crab legs as well as oysters. Nick has opened another place at 7429 W. Addison. It's three times the size of Portside and loses the cozy, old barroom feeling. Papo, the cook, headed the kitchen at the Half Shell on

Diversey for a long time. If you want a full meal, and your partner only wants a drink, belly up to the bar here.

4pm-2am, $, 65¢/$1, 14 wines $4-$7, 1 dom/1 imp, juke.

The Pump Room

1301 N. State Pkwy.   266-0360
Ambassador East Hotel
Lettuce Entertain You Enterprise, prop.

To get into the Pump Room, enter on the Goethe Street side of the Ambassador East, shuffle up the stairs and take a left. You'll find a narrow corridor lined with hundreds of photographs of the celebrities who have walked this way. Over the years, practically every star of one kind or another has been here. The old Pump Room, which went bankrupt/defunct in 1975, was remodeled and reopened by the Lettuce Entertain You people in July of 1976. There is a small controversy in Chicago about the aesthetic quality of that change. The old Pump Room, in its declining years, was certainly getting worn and shabby. It was a faded continental elegance, with paintings and tapestries, that many people miss, even if it was tattered on the edges.

The new decor is formal Lettuce hip. Wooden panelled walls, white tablecloths and glistening stemware are in the dining room. The bar is square, stolid and serious, the bar stools are covered with a velvet-like fabric, and as you sit here, you overlook the dining room. There's a piano and cafe table area off to the side, and during cocktail hour they serve one of the city's best free buffets. Good brands of bar booze are served and there's an excellent selection of rare liqueurs. The best possible beers are offered: Heineken, Lowenbrau, Beck's dark, Michelob, Carta Blanca, Pilsener Urquell and Miller Lite. There are 65 wines ranging from $7 to $58, and a menu of specialty drinks, "the Spiritual Guideline"—Lettuce E.Y. can't offer fruit frappes or ice cream swirled with liqueurs without throwing a pun in.

The place was named, back in 1938, after an elegant tea house in Bath, England where society people broke tradition and mingled with actors. Which reminds me that the word bar comes from the French *barrier,* literally barrier or table-topped fence used in road-houses to keep the commoner scum away from the French nobility.

The staff at the Pump Room is friendly and intelligent, and the bartender went so far as to ask me, "Shall I pour your beer for you, sir?" He knew that knowledgeable and serious beer drinkers may well not want anyone mucking with the bottle and glass, perhaps getting the foam off by critical millimeters. The beer is served with iced pilsner glasses, a bar treat. There's reel to reel "easy listening" music, live music at night, and the windows on the far wall overlook State Parkway.

The Pump Room is still elegant, but certainly different from the days when Chicago was the nation's rail hub, when celebrities strolled in formal dress, when Booth Number One was an important social institution. But you should make your own evaluation of what amounts to the death of an era. The bar is still a bar, there's talk about yesterday's ball game and about somebody who made a complete ass of himself the night before. And it's still the Pump Room. But (there's something sad about how history moves) the bar is covered with some incredibly deceptive linoleum-stuff. It looks like mahogany.

11:30-2 Sun-Thurs, Fri & Sat later, $$, $1.50/$2.00, # 5-7:30 hors d'ouevres, 2 dom/5 imp, live cabaret music 7 nights.

The Pumping Company

6157 N. Broadway   743-7994
Jim Vann & Frank Thoma, props.

How would you like to play a bowling machine where a little man rolls a ball bearing ball for you? Or test your strength on a machine? Do you have the urge to see 10 little mechanical men strike up the band and play for you? Ever play the Iron Claw crane where you grab a toy or a mess of sand that dribbles away? Do you miss those Museum of Science and Industry "metal typers" that put your name on an aluminum coin? Or, do you want to fulfill that fantasy and (dream of all drinker's dreams) rent a POST OFFICE MAIL BOX RIGHT IN A BAR!!!

All of these thrills and more are to be found at the Pumping Company. It might sound like an amusement park, but it looks like a bar and these gimcracks don't intrude on your drinking pleasure.

Named after a line in an old poem about the Chicago fire, The Pumping Company is a new Rogers Park bar which is comfortable, well designed, and certainly interesting. Two higher levels near the front windows are quiet and offer room for chatting, while the basement holds another bar and a fireplace. The wood in the place was once a southern Illinois barn.

The patrons are generally 25 to 35 years old, an "even" crowd, and Friday nights are a favorite. It's then that the oldies 45 rpm record collection comes out. They have 2500 + records from the 1930's through the 70's.

Bring your nickels and quarters.

3pm-2, $, 65¢/$1.00, # 3-8, 2 dom/1 imp, games galore, juke & dj.

The Quiet Night

953 W. Belmont   348-7100
Richard Harding, prop.

The Quiet Night is a traditional Chicago popular music room. Linda Ronstat, John Denver, Chris Christoffersen, the late Jim Croce, Carly Simon, Chic Corea, Herbi Hancock, Louden Wainwright, Dave Van Ronk, and a whole lot of other people have performed here. The music room is a comfortably sized L-shaped affair with the stage in the corner, so there's hardly a bad seat. It's the stage, tables, and an impressive bank of stained glass windows overlooking the street. That's what the place is about and it's all you need.

You enter next door to the Belmont L station and climb a steep flight of stairs to get to the Quiet Night. The music room is to the right, and to the left there's a small bar and a comfortable room with two pool tables. This room is used by a small number of locals who appreciate a quiet place to play.

Richard Harding has been one of the Near North's bar frontiersmen for some years. The Quiet Night was on Wells Street 8 years ago. Before that Harding had Poor Richard's on Sedgewick and before that Mother Blues. He's struggled with the high pricing dilemma that small clubs have with name acts and has tried to keep things equitable. The cover charge varies with each act, but you'll be spending a good bit of money throughout a night here.

8pm-2, $$, $1.00/$1.50, 1 dom/3 imp, pool, live music.

Ragtime Inn

5946 W. Grand Ave.   622-4892
Martin Maylan, prop.

Marty Maylan has gone to a lot of trouble to create a bar that people will want to come to. The decor is modern, with fresh wood-panelled and white walls, framed prints, marquee light bulbs above the bar and a sense of spaciousness and cleanliness about the place. There's a back room that's darker and used as a dining area, and it has large glass doors opening to a beer garden.

Maylan keeps a stiff check on the front door, demanding 3 i.d.'s, "proper attire" and a "21 or over" policy which reserves the place for the older drinkers and keeps the hordes of kids at bay.

Sandwiches, burgers and dinners are served. It's comfortable, popular, and elegant for a neighbhorhood place. You can stroll from the Ragtime across the street to hit Durty Dick's or down the block to Smiler Coogan's if you're in a pub crawl mood.

11:30-2, $, 60¢/$1, no #, 5 dom/2 imp, pinball, juke box.

Ray's Bleachers

3655 N. Sheffield   DI8-9139
Ray Meyer, prop.

Under the scoreboard, across from Wrigley Field's rear-end bleacher gates, squats Ray's Bleachers, home of the left-field bleacher bums. The place, although it looks like a garage (and maybe because it does), is a Chicago tradition. This is where the serious beer-swilling bleacher fans (those who scorn box seats for the lack of cultural stimulation they offer) begin their day around 9:30 or 10 in the morning before a game and end it towards 11pm.

Ray's is filled with cases of pop, beer and assorted merchandise. Baseball photos, pennants, pins and memorabilia cover the walls like a mold growth, and a rowdy but fun atmosphere fills the air as countless fans jam their way in.

On game days they serve hotdogs, hamburgers and Polish sausage to get in the way of the hogsheads of beer guzzled here. When you feel sporty and want to approach Wrigley Field from the bleachers' side of life, stop at Ray's first.

noon-11pm (game days 9:30am-11pm), ¢, 70¢/70¢, 4 dom/0 imp, pool & pinball, juke.

Redford's Saloon

2548 N. Halsted   549-1250
Lee Stanley, prop.

Jazz is making a strong comeback in Chicago, and in the last year two jazz clubs have opened on the Near North side within a few blocks of each other. Colette's is over on Lincoln Avenue and Redford's has recently opened its doors on Halsted Street. It's a well designed place, but more important, it picks some of the best jazz musicians available locally. Everything is clean and new, decorated with white stucco, dark wood, framed prints and antiques. They have a piano from 1906 that sounds clear as a bell, and the room isn't so large that you can get a bad seat. Judy Roberts, Jody Christian, Danny Long and Streetdancer have been booked. Unlike Colette's, there's usually a one dollar cover charge, but drinks are reasonably priced and the first set starts early, at 8 p.m.

4pm-2, $, $1/$1.25, # 4-7, 3 dom/4 imp, live jazz 7 nights.

Resi's Bierstube

2034 W. Irving Park   472-1749
Herbert Stober, prop.

Ah, here it is. Chicago's great Bavarian bierstube, on Irving Park, just west of Lincoln Avenue.

As authentically German as you'll find in the States, Resi's is a joy to the drinker. The list of 48 imported beers, almost all German, creates a graduate program in drinking. The beer garden is simple, yet lovely. Grape vines (yes, with real grapes) cover the garden, a friendly tree shades it, and there are flowers growing here and there. There's a bratwurst-thuringer-knackwurst-potato salad-sauerkraut menu which comes from a home-style clean, and I mean *clean* kitchen.

Resi's sells more weissbier (4 different brands) than any other place in the city. In case you're not familiar with it, weissbier is a light German beer (somewhat bitter) served in a huge liter glass with either fresh lemon, raspberry syrup, or a green liqueur called wald-meister.

The decor is collectors-Germanic. Helmets, medals, military insignia, bric-a-brac, and other curiosities cover the walls. Sausage and hard-boiled eggs are behind the bar, and (this is what makes America beautiful) the bartender's name is Pepe.

I strong recommend a summer evening in the beer garden where you can sip, watch the grapes grow and observe grade school-age girls bus the tables with awesome efficiency.

CAUTION: Closed on Mondays, kitchen closed on Sunday, beer garden closes at midnight.

2pm-2am, ¢, 50¢/75c, no #, 6 German wines, 5 dom/ 48 imp, foosball (?), piped-in German FM musak.

Riccardo's

437 N. Rush St.   WH4-8815
Nick Angelo

The downstairs was Kelly's Stable and the upstairs was a speakeasy, in what was then a working class neighborhood behind the Wrigley Building. Frame buildings and houses sat next to each other on the street that ran down to the river. In 1934 Rick Riccardo, who was an artist, opened the doors of Riccardo's, a restaurant and bar. The room that is now the northernmost was the original dining room, and where the kitchen now is the bar stood. In the original dining room you can see the murals that Riccardo painted there himself. The walls in the center room, built in 1939, also have examples of Riccardo's art.

Riccardo's is one of the classic Chicago traditions. It used to cater to artists and neighborhood people in the 30's, but it grew more and more elegant, till now it's one of those internationally famous places for internationally famous drinkers. Michigan Avenue people come here as well as a good number of writers and reporters from Chicago's dailies.

Rick Riccardo came here from Italy and kept a tradition of outdoor cafe tables at his bar. Today you'll still find outdoor seating in clement weather. Charles Bianchi, a kind and elderly man, has worked for Riccardo's since the beginning and is still there. He'll be able to show you what was where 40 years ago. On Thursday and Friday nights there are strolling musicians, and, oh yes, the bar is curved in the shape of a painter's palette.

11:30-11pm, $, $1.00/$1.25, 28 wines $5-$20, 2 dom/1 imp.

Rick's Cafe Americain

644 N. Lake Shore Dr.   943-9200
Holiday Inn, prop.

Holiday Inn has spent a lot of money to create a simulated version of Humphrey Bogart's cabaret in *Casablanca.* It's not an exact replica, but it evokes the quality of the film's club. It's located on the first floor of the Holiday Inn, and as you approach, the decor begins to take over. Palms, mounted brass plateware, stuccoed walls and doorways arched in the shape of the spade in a deck of cards. At the entrance there's a free-standing cut-out of Bogart which can be startlingly life-like. Rattan chairs, Moroccan tiles on the walls and bar top, tapestries and revolving fans fill out the design while the waitresses weave about in desert-hooded costumes. The cafe features live music, jazz greats, some of them from the nearly-forgotten past.

I think everyone should give it a try, at least for the visual experience. Bring a film buff or a Bogie fan.

The Pinnacle Lounge is on the 33rd floor of the same building, and it offers a nice view of the city to the south and west. This is adjacent to the restaurant that revolves. Rumor has it that the whole 33rd floor revolves, but only the center floor of the restaurant does. In the Pinnacle you can sit in overstuffed leatherette chairs and for $2 a drink watch the city sit still.

Rick's: 8pm-2am, closed Sun & Mon, $$ but no cover, no minimum, $2/$2.25, no #, 1 dom/1 imp, no games (except for an unused simulated casino table), live jazz.

River Shannon

425 W. Armitage   944-5087
A. Wollsey, B. & J. Nordham, props.

This is a Near North neighborhood tavern for young junior executives. The men wear suits after work and look like they went to Notre Dame, chic rough-and-ready lawyers, brokers, bankers, etc. They guzzle cases of Irish whiskey every week and fill the River Shannon.

The bar is as Irish as anything is after the third generation, which is not much. It's a very good looking place
with a great dark wood back bar, and there's an antique
wooden cooler, stained glass, antiques and mirrors.
They have a free popcorn machine and, blessedly, no
juke box. The music is taped.

Should you not like the well-dressed singles crowd at
night, I recommend the place during the day for
peaceful and pleasant sipping.

Mon-Fri 2-2, Sat & Sun noon-closing, $, 65¢/$1.25, # 4-8
M-F, 4 dom/4 imp, pinball, tapes.

The Rusty Scupper

1750 N. Clark (in The Warehouse)   944-3131
Borel Restaurant Corp., prop.

The Rusty Scupper is owned by a restaurant corporation
that has over 19 outlets around the country in Boston,
San Francisco, Ohio and other places. In Chicago
they've created one of the new wave of tasteful, designed
bars. Somewhere along the line, the aesthetics of this
split from the traditional Chicago bar has to be brought
to question. The conservative hard liners want a family
operation tavern, one with limited and clearly defined
social boundaries. These places have their comforts and
their drawbacks. The other end of the scale is the
designers' antique-cum-art 70's where the place and its
patrons are part of a visual showcase. It's always fun to
view collector's items, but can you *relax* while drinking
in a gallery-fashion show? I've observed the problem in
Arnie's, which is Chicago's current high fashion bar.
Everybody and everything is so tasteful that you can
sense a discomfort with it all in the air. This is, after all,
still Chicago. However, the aesthetics of salooning will
be the source of unending debate. You can get no con-
sensus when dealing with an art form and the "best bar"
battle inevitably degenerates into a jungle of taste. The
only true, accurate and purely objective viewpoint is, of
course, my opinion.

The Rusty Scupper is one of the more pleasant
attempts at the new art of the fashion bar. The secret is, I

think, that the designers (and these places *always* have designers) didn't try to overdo it. The building itself is the restored 100-year-old Kennelly furniture warehouse, and you can see the original walls and ceiling with their massive beams intact.

There's a copper-topped bar, hardwood floors and brick walls. The lighting is done nicely, not too bright, and there's some of the inevitable stained glass hanging around. The lower level is the restaurant, there are two levels of bars above it, with the main bar in the middle. The top bar has entertainment on Friday and Saturday nights, usually folk or quieter rock acts. You'll find couches on the top level and a wall of windows on the east side of each floor, presenting a nice view of Lincoln Park.

11:30-2am, $, 65¢/$1.25, # 5-7, 18 wines in dining room, 3 dom/2 imp, no games, stereo.

Sage's East

181 E. Lake Shore Dr.   944-1557
Gene Sage, prop.

In the Lake Shore Drive Hotel, across from the Oak Street beach, you will find Sage's East. It's a dark cocktail lounge kind of bar with padded booths, a piano bar, and a decor that primarily relies on dim lighting. There's a big singles scene after 5, and a wide range of people of all ages, most of whom look like they shop at I. Magnin. There are lots of three piece suits, gold jewelry and furs. Jackets are required for the gentlemen, and since even the bartenders are in formal wear it makes sense. Despite this air of fashion, there's a television set over the bar, a mundane touch which seems out of place. Free hors d'oeuvres are served and Sage's wine list numbers over 200 wines. Back at the turn of the century, the Lake Shore Drive was an elegant hotel, it had an elegant bar and, later, an elegant speakeasy. Sage's East has inherited this tradition.

11:30-2, $$, $1.25/$1.75, 200 wines $6-$375, 2 dom/ 1 imp, piano 5-closing.

Sam's Working Man's Palace

4400 W. Diversey
Sam, prop.

Sam's Working Man's Palace ranks with Wally's Polish Pump Room and the Baby Doll Polka Lounge. Needless to say, it's a dump, but with a name like that it deserves attention. It's ancient, half bar-half liquor store, with stacks of beer, soda, barrels and cases against the walls. The decor is hard core economical, from the cinder block walls and cement floor to the plank and linoleum bar. There's a prehistoric wooden beer cooler with brass fittings and the bartenders wear white aprons. It's cheap, it's a neighborhood place, there's nothing extraordinary about it, except its name.

¢.

Schaller's Pump

3714 S. Halsted
Schaller Family, prop.

Enter with reverence. Located across the street from the 11th Ward regular Democratic offices, Schaller's Pump has stood as the home tavern of the Bridgeport politicoes for over 80 years. The fourth generation of the Schaller family works here now, and as you sit at the bar you can only guess which monumental political decisions were made right here, at the Daley boys' saloon. The corny "if walls could talk" image comes to mind. It's a walk away from Mayor Daley's home, down the street from Our Lady of the Nativity church, where the Mayor went regularly to worship.

It's an old, old, worn bar. The ages and generations of Irish drinkers have left their marks on its surface. There's nothing fancy or elegant here, it's a bare boards operation with covered tables and a simple, home-cooked menu. Nowadays it's quiet, a steady flow of drinkers seem to sip rather than toss them down. On the walls are arches made with bull ropes from the stockyards, again only a few blocks away.

You can only think of Richard J. Daley when you're here. You can see the ghosts, the cigar smoke, the conversations, the deals, the Last Hurrah, all of it before you. It's cheap, simple, worn, and full of history. If you're Irish and from the Southside of Chicago, this is the kind of place your grandfather would have owned. In the men's room there's the most curiously touching bit of graffitti I've ever seen and it does what is perhaps the best job of summing up Schaller's, Bridgeport and Daley. It simply says, "Love your mother."

Schulein's

2100 W. Irving Park   IR8-2100
Charles Schulein, prop.

In 1886 great-grandfather Joe Schulein started his first saloon on the corner of Randolph and LaSalle. It was called the Quincy No. 9. The second saloon was opened in 1910 on the corner of Halsted and Willow. That crumbling building is still standing. During Prohibition, Joe said to his sons Matt and Ed, "Go downstairs young men, go downstairs." And they went into the Speakeasy business. Schulein's weathered the tough depression years and became a popular spot for servicemen home on leave during WWII. In 1948 they moved to Irving Park Road and the third generation, Ed and Charley, took over. Now Charley runs the place with his son Bob. This makes it Chicago's oldest one-family operation.

Today you'll find the original Volstead Act "CLOSED" sign framed in Schulein's. This is a citation from the U.S. District Court telling Matt he had done wrong during the Years of Darkness. The present bar was also a speakeasy and is 77 years old. During Prohibition the policy was "a wide open side door."

The bar is handsome, elegant and comfortable, as befits the home of the alcohol revolutionaries of our nation's history.

Schulein's is also a restaurant with a full American menu, white linens and a family atmosphere, but as a bar, it is a study in quiet elegance. A beautiful back bar has been sitting where it is now since 1900, the bar itself a pleasure to lean on. Stained glass, plants, antiques and a mess of old Chicago memorabilia are arranged around the place. Free cheese and crackers are served to drinkers, and five nights a week there's a piano player plunking away. The side windows, which are set high, open to a row of trees on the east, which is a pleasant sight.

Is that enough? No. From Matt unto Ed and Charley, and unto the next generation of Bob, a tradition of card tricks has been passed. So, today you can find one of the Schuleins behind the bar, in vest, shirt and tie, wowing the citizens with a repertoire from "Pick a card, any card," to the "flying cards" stunt which is immortalized in an oil painting showing Matt with a whirling deck. Schulein's is a short block from Resi's Bierstube and both should be on the itinerary of anyone who seriously wishes to sip, imbibe, or drink in this city.

11:30-1am, $, 75¢/$1.25, 30 wines $5-$20, 2 dom/3 imp, piano bar 5 nights.

Scot's

7242 N. Damen, at Rogers Ave. 743-1800
Scotty Colia

Four and a half years ago it was a National Tea grocery, now it's a piano bar-supper club with the advantage of having a grocery store's parking lot. The bar is dark and done in that black naugahyde lounge look. The booths are arranged at different levels and the bar has two levels, one side has regular sized bar stools and the other has chairs. This allows just about everyone to have a good view of the piano player. Scot's books a series of the better "easy listening" piano bar performers, and they play 4 nights a week. As a supper club Scot's serves prime rib, steaks, chicken and seafood. There are specialty ice cream drinks for $1.50 and a series of "coffee international" drinks. The atmosphere is subdued and the patrons tend towards middle age, but anyone is welcome for quiet lounge-style drinking.

5pm-2am, Sun 11am-2 & 5pm-10pm, $, 80¢/$1.20, 10 wines $4.50 & up, 4 dom/1 imp, juke, fm, piano bar from 8pm Thurs-Sat.

Second City

1616 N. Wells St.   DE7-3992
Bernard Sahlins, prop.

If you've heard of improvisational theater at Second City, but have had a hard time making reservations, paying the admission and getting there on time, here's the answer for you:
    Tues, Wed, Thurs, Sun—11pm
    Fri & Sat—1am
At these times you can stroll right into Second City, wihout paying a penny for admission, and watch the improvisation part of the performances. The actors, having taken suggestions from the audience, create and perform scenes right before your very eyes.

Amazingly, a high proportion of the regular paying customers leave during the intermission before this part of the show and their seats wait for you. Service is slow because, instead of doing cash and carry, the waitresses have to run checks on everyone, and they're always in a flurry to collect. Order two drinks at a time. The cheese snack is decent, and the humor is excellent. Monday night, the Second City Touring Company does a revue ($1.50) with no reservations required.

Shari's

2901 N. Clark   348-9599

Shari's is a Near North gay men's neighborhood bar. It's been around for quite a while and was once at the top of the list, but the proliferation of gay bars has slowed things down just a bit. One thing about the place is that, at any time of the day, there are people in the place. Many of the gay bars open late and start filling up later, but at Shari's there's a full crowd, day or night. It's carpeted, simply designed with brick walls and mirrors. A casual place for gay men to go.

Noon-2am, no pricing available, 2 dom/0 imp, no games, juke.

Sheahan's

11136 S. Western Ave.   233-2334
Mrs. Eileen Sheahon, prop.

Sheahon's is a popular family operation on the far Southside. It's a large, clean and well designed bar which serves primarily young people, with a slant towards those of Irish descent. The walls are cream colored, framed prints are hung about, and dark wood prevails at tables and booths. The most comforting aspect of this effect is that decorations are not overdone, as they so often are. Prices are cheap, sandwiches and cheese and crackers are served. Because the place is tastefully simple, miraculously without any games, it is a more than usually social bar, and on the weekends they pack them in.

11am-2am, ¢, 50¢/80¢, 6 dom/1 imp, juke & stereo.

Shenanigan's

16 W. Division   642-2344
T. Gorusch, G. Maresca, & P. Henke, props.

Shenanigan's is running a neck and neck race with its next door neighbor, Butch Maguire's, for the city's singles bar championship. It's here that young well dressed people come to meet each other. The social order is well established in a casual boy meets girl way, and while the traditional no-frills drinker avoids places like this, thousands of people are attracted to Shenanigan's every week. When newcomers to the city are "looking for action" this is where they usually wind up, within stein throwing distance of Maguire's and Mother's.

Shenanigan's is big, full of antiques, stained glass, dark wood, Tiffany et cetera, and there's a nice skylight at the rear of the second room. During the day you'll find it friendly and spacious, lunches are served and there's a brunch menu on weekends. At night you'll find it filled with young up-and-coming, mainstream Americans. The people who run the place are congenial. They don't give you that paramilitary club feeling that other Rush Street area places do (with everyone in some kind of uniform), and for the history books, Shenanigan's was a Chicago pioneer in hiring women bartenders.

11-2am, $, 75¢/$1.25, # M-F 6-8pm, 3 dom/2 imp, pinball, electronic, juke & FM.

Sherlock's Home

900 N. Michigan Ave.   787-0545
Canteen Corp, props.

"When will you be pleased to dine, Mr. Holmes?" asked Mrs. Hudson his housekeeper.

"Seven thirty the day after tomorrow," Holmes replied.

This and other quotes of the famous Holmes are printed on chalk boards throughout his "home." The place, which is quite large, has two levels and three rooms. Downstairs is the den, with fireplace, large wing-backed leather chairs, chandelier, lamps, and carpeting. Sherlock's is an imaginative reproduction of Holmes' home, down to the knife collection on the mantlepiece. If the whole idea sounds too cute to you, give it a try anyway, at least for the sensation of plopping into a huge stuffed chair while drinking out. The location, on Michigan Avenue, makes it a perfect oasis when you find yourself frayed from the urban experience.

The place has an all-woman staff, and there is a menu of sandwiches, snacks and appetizers, shrimp, oysters, brie cheese with fruits, or perhaps you'd enjoy "Inspector Lestrade's favorite."

All in all, Sherlock's is an impressive accomplishment of concept and design. Wandering in from Michigan Avenue can be confusing, so there's also a Delaware Street entrance.

11:30-2, $, 90¢/$1.50, 50 wines, 2 dom/3 imp, variety of taped music.

Shinnick's

3758 S. Union
Celine Shinnick, prop.

Shinnick's has been at 3758 South Union for over 90 years, it's always been a tavern, and the back bar is one of the oldest and most beautiful in the city. John L. Sullivan used to hang out here with dozens of other boxers, and the number of Bridgeport politicoes who have passed through Shinnick's doors gave it the name "Little City Hall". It's been in the family now for 43 years, and the third generation works behind the bar.

A while back, business took a slump, but the young people of Bridgeport adopted the place as their own, and now they jam in on weekends and on school vacations from college. The prices are rock bottom, there's a pool table, color tv, junk food, a carryout cooler and a mess of candy for the kids who troop in and out with their nickels and dimes. On Saint Patrick's Day and opening day at Sox Park there's complete bedlam here, as there is everywhere in the neighborhood.

The back bar is worth a trip, just to look at. It's a huge, black mahogany affair, with carved columns that bring a soft whistle of appreciation from the bar afficionado. Its mirrors are vast and they are the original glass, never having been (knock on wood) smashed in a brawl.

9am-2am, ¢, 40¢/50¢, 6 dom/1 imp, pool table, juke.

The Sign of the Trader

lobby level of the Board of Trade Building
141 W. Jackson   427-3443
Jack Bolling, prop.

The Chicago Board of Trade is, in many ways, the kitchen of the world. It's here that the foodstuffs of America are bought and sold as commodities. The Sign of the Trader is the bar where *many* of the people involved in this business go to calm their nerves. On the 5th floor there's a visitors' observatory where you can look down to the 4th floor pits where the commodities are traded with a frighteningly insane frenzy of hand gestures, violent movements and hysterical message sending. The system works, but its overwhelming sense of human frailty will frighten you. Down at the Trader, the food and booze is pumped out at much the same hectic rate. Bunker-Ramo quote machines are mounted to give instant reports on the market's fluctuations so nobody misses a beat. Wheels, deals, speculation, elation and regret go on here. The market closes at 1:30pm, so all of this goes on early in the day. Across the street you'll find the Brokers Inn, which is the more low key and casual place for trading people to go.

11:00-8:30 Mon-Fri only, $, 75¢/$1.30, 1 dom.

Single File

934 W. Webster   525-1558
Chuck Bellak, prop.

The Single File, situated in DePaul University's back yard, has a standard college bar feeling about it. The main room, which could be attractive, is jammed with games and the college-age patrons plug their quarters in and ping away. Thursday is 25c beer day; burgers, sandwiches and salads are served.

Besides the bar room there's a music room where live performances are held seven nights a week during the fall-through-spring school year. At the rear there's a surprisingly pleasant beer garden with plenty of greenery and tables set on a brick walk. The beer garden isn't used extensively and it has a nice semi-private feeling about it.

11am-2am, ¢, 50¢/$1.00, # 4-6, 4 dom/1 imp, many games, juke and live music.

Skyline Lounge

1004 W. Belmont   LI9-9395
Emmett Morin, prop.

The Skyline has been a near-North country and western music bar for over 15 years. The music is good, and the dance floor scene is pure Kentucky. The bar traveler will find this to be the more "authentic" of the country places in Chicago, combined with a disciplined, well-run and friendly bar operation.
   Yes, you can see cowboys in cowboy hats and the ladies dressed in their weekend going-dancing finery. You can go dancing in blue jeans here and not worry about someone's concept of a dress code. The lack of a good imported beer is my only lament here. The Nashville Cats, the house band, are playing at the Skyline, so get ready to tap your feet when you go in.

3pm-4am, $, $1.25/$1.25, no #, 2 dom/0 imp, bowling game, C/W.

Slowik's

3200 N. Milwaukee   AV3-9595
Socrates Tingas, prop.

Slowik's is the city's great, traditional neighborhood tavern/cafeteria. It's been on north Milwaukee Avenue for over 40 years and was called Slowik's International Grill in the early days. They sell their own brand of horseradish. When you want horseradish to go, and a beer while you're placing your order, this is the place. Slowik's Delight comes in the regular and beet flavored variety and its 80c a jar. It's so famous that Mister Joe's notable tavern carries it and sells it on Rush Street.

The building is one of those triangular structures formed by the angling of Milwaukee Avenue so you enter at the small corner and the place expands away from you. To your left is a venerable bar which is 60 feet long, and to your right there's a series of tables and a steam table where the food is served. Huge schooners of Budweiser go for 55c, and Michelob is 65c. For 16 oz. that's more than a fair price. It's a Polish, German, Irish, Scandinavian neighborhood place with all kinds of people who come for simple pleasures. There's a hall in the back used by local unions for their meetings. The hall is equipped with a '30's hardwood masterpiece bar.

They watch tv at Slowik's, eat daily specials from $1.75, munch pretzels, and it's the kind of tavern that Mike Royko probably knows about and loves.

7am-midnight, ¢, 55¢/65¢, 10 dom/1 imp.

Smiler Coogan's

5637 W. Grand   889-9809
Tom & Mike Gioia, props.

Out on Grand Avenue, there's a strip of popular bars, including Durty Dick's and Smiler Coogan's. Coogan's is a casual place where neighborhood people drink. The interior is a woodworker's dream. The Gioia brothers and their father are all carpenters who put the place together themselves using generous amounts of light colored wood, cultured stone and brick. There's a handsome bar, and comfortable street watching windows. There are the usual tavern games, a juke box and pizza is served. As a local spot, the place can claim no unusual attraction, but it is a comfortable and pleasant place to drink.

noon-2, $, 60¢/$1.00, # noon-8, 6 dom/1 imp, games, juke.

Somebody Else's Troubles

2470 N. Lincoln Ave.   953-0660
Henry Nathan & Bill Redhed, props.

The Troubles, named from the lyrics of a Steve Goodman
song, is a first rate folk music club. It's visually pleasant,
with brick walls, dark wood, and a handsome back bar
imported from England. Ed and Fred Holstein, Chicago
performers, run the place and you can hear Tom Paxton,
Dave Van Ronk, Mike Seeger, Utah Phillips, and Rosalie
Sorrels. A fandom of local musicians perform here as
well and Fred Holstein is the mainstay singer.

When a big name singer appears at Troubles, they'll
sell tickets, but usually there's a cover, varying from
$1.50 to $4.00, and a 2 drink minimum. The Earl of Old
Town and Barbarossa are the other two top folk clubs in
the city, but Troubles is the most pleasant place to sit.
Service, as it always seems to be in folk joints, can be
indifferent. My theory is that all the waitresses in these
places are folkies themselves, with a guitar in the back
room, ready to jump on the stage should the performer
suddenly step into a space/time portal and disappear.
Or maybe they just think

It ain't hard to get along
With Somebody Else's Troubles
As long as fate is busting
Someone else's bubbles

4pm-2am, $, $1/$1.50, # 4-9, 3 dom/3 imp, live folk.

Sonny's Inn

3104 E. 91st St.   221-0261
Sonny & Loretta Grzetich, props.

It sits next to the railroad tracks on a commercial street,
but it looks like a roadhouse you'd find in the country.
The bar has that same away-from-it feeling too. The
place is comfortably worn and ancient as only a bar can
get in 34 years, and you can settle in here. Like most of
the places in this part of town, Sonny's does a strong
home-cooking business, with Sonny himself doing the

kitchen work. There's a nice long bar, padded stools, and a bunch of collectibles and knick-knacks hung about the walls. You can get a draught Heineken to go with the special hamburger that's a pride of Sonny's, and you will eat cheaply and well. The patrons are neighborhood regulars, and a conversational, friendly air is found here. The most unusual aspect of the place is their hours. They open at 6am and close at 8pm, and they're closed on Saturday and Sunday—that tells you, more than anything, what Sonny's is about.

Mon-Fri 6am-8pm, $.

Sterch's

2238 N. Lincoln Ave.   281-9683
Harlan Stern & Robert Smerch, props.

Sterch's has made it on the strength of its funkiness and its personnel. Here, in the middle of the Lincoln Avenue "club" strip, we find a neighborhood tavern where the street's bartenders come to cool off. During the day, Harlan is behind the bar, ready to discuss any and all issues, especially baseball. Bob Smerch, once a carnival barker, is renowned for his carrot auction on the street during the Spring Festival of the Arts. He wears a bunny or clown costume for the affair. These are men you want to serve you a drink. When you come to their bar, cluttered as it is with beer cases, kegs and vital junk, you feel that you are welcome and that they like you, an important consideration in a Chicago bar.

Carrots are plentiful in the Sterch's design. That's because they serve the city's only (to my knowledge) french fried carrots. Give the carrots or the chili a try and reconsider your concept of bar food.

One wall is devoted to scheduled displays of the work of local artists. Every spring, though, that space is dedicated to a display of each of that year's baseball cards. 1977 had 660 cards sans chewing gum. Perhaps the best summary came from Harlan: "The place is due for remodelling and we're not gonna."

11am-2am, ¢, 60¢/$1, # 2-7 weekday, 3 dom/7 imp, pinball, bowling, funky juke.

Sweetwater

1028 N. Rush   787-5552
D. Buffone, S. Lombardo, B. Marsico, props.

Sweetwater is one of the Rush Street high fashion bars. The bar is an oval that sits beneath a large oval skylight, chandeliers hang over the bartender, and you look across elegantly set tables to a wall of windows which show the street beyond. As a restaurant, Sweetwater offers one of those vast multinational menus that have become so popular. Here you can go from Pate of Pheasant with truffles and pistachios to the Singapore burger. The death of ethnic bars in Chicago may come as the hip restaurants continue to offer food from many nations and the genuine family-run places disappear. No one will need to travel to Chinatown or the Hungarian restaurant when their foods can be found in the nearest fashionable restaurant-bar.

Nonetheless, Sweetwater has good food of all kinds. It's pleasantly elegant and it has several very nice touches. The tables and chairs are wicker, there are large mirrors, a red tiled floor, stucco pillars and couches on one side of cocktail tables, chairs on the other. The effect is uncluttered. Like many good looking bars, it's best when it's not full.

The patrons are the Rush Street business set, Rush Street Romeos and young lovelies dressed in their finest. Cocktail hour and weekends are their busiest times. One of the dining areas is called the Pelican room. Can people who run a Pelican room be at all bad?

11:30-1am, weekends 2am, $$, $1.50/$2, 5:30-7 hors d'ouevres, 151 wines $7.50-$600, 2 dom/2 imp, taped music.

The Swiss Inn

4541 N. Western   271-2490
Bob & Erna Nicholson

The Swiss Inn is one of the city's finest saloons. In the tradition of family taverns and restaurants, the Swiss Inn welcomes workers, executives, old folks and kids. It's homey, comfortable and not fancy. There's a restaurant menu, half German, half American, with prime rib, Bar B Q ribs, and sandwiches. Mr. Nicholson, in keeping with the continued social stirring of the city, plays ethnic records from several nations. "Lots of Irish," he says, "They like it."

The bar is decorated in a knick-knack German style which helps create the atmosphere of a family-run operation. There are ten imported beers including a weissbier, and a German wine list. Give the place a try.

11am-midnight, $, 60¢/$1.00, 3 dom/10 imp, ethnic records.

Sybaris Lounge

875 N. Michigan Ave. (96th floor)   787-9599
ARA Services, prop.

Rather than pay the Observatory people their fee to ride to the top of the John Hancock Center, you can go to the Chestnut Street side of the building, ride to the Sybaris Lounge on the 96th floor, pay to have a drink and see the same spectacular view of the city.

This is the highest bar in Chicago and it is named after the ancient Greek city in southern Italy, noted for its wealth and luxury. Sybaris was destroyed in 510 B.C. Needless to say the modern sky-high version has nothing to do with that ancient city in motif, decor or purpose.

There are small tables, comfortable lounge chairs, a bar and the windows, which is what it's all about. You can sit there and gaze, find your childhood playground, watch hi-rise swimmers, the ant-sized people crawling below, the great midwestern horizon. The clientele is touristy, but relax anyway and enjoy the vista. When in Sybaris, do as the Sybarites.

Noon-1am, $$, $1.75/$2.50, 2 dom/1 imp, popular live music 7pm-1am.

Sylvester's

2700 N. Lincoln Ave.   929-6840
Sylvester Klish, Jr.

From the outside Sylvester's looks like a bar that's been converted from a Chicken Box that was converted from a gas station. It looks that way because that's what happened.

Today, Sylvester Klish is trying something new in Chicago which is working successfully in other U.S. cities, the comedy club. Working on the theory that there are plenty of music bars in the city, and there are, Sylvester's is presenting a series of nightly comedy acts. Stand-up comedians, comic musicians and improvisational theatre companies are the fare. So, in an informal atmosphere you can see, for example, Second City style performances that take you away on flights of fancy. Between shows you can lean back and speculate on the former location of chicken fryers. I think the car lifts were over there . . . no . . . maybe . . .

6pm-2am, $, $1/$1.50, no #, 3 dom/0 imp, pinball, juke.

Tally Ho Lounge

1951 W. Howard   465-9259
Don Pooler, prop.

The Tally Ho Lounge is right across the street from Evanston, which is a town dry enough to serve drinks only with meals and doesn't have a single saloon. It's a neighborhood bar where you can watch a ball game or shoot pool. The Tally Ho is honorary Fire Station Number Six of the Evanston Fire Department (which has five stations). The Boltwood College Alumni Association, a pack of middle-aged ex-athletes who used to play some mean ball at Boltwood Park, holds reunions here. At night it's a college bar where Northwestern and Loyola students hang out.

But in spite of the tavern's many identities, it remains unpretentious and Chicago-like. The bar banter is sports fan, and the local college athletes gravitate here. It's a big place, rowdy and friendly. Large wooden beams hold it up. College pennants and the usual tavern paraphernalia cover the walls.

The name, The Tally Ho Lounge, is quite a joke since no one knows where it came from or why it's used. You couldn't sell tickets to a fox hunt here, but once you explained the game, you'd be sure to pick up a few bets on the outcome.

9am-2, ¢, 50¢/70¢, no #, 7 dom/1 imp, pool and pinball, juke box.

Tango

3172 N. Sheridan   935-0350
George Badonsky, prop.

The Tango is a fine seafood restaurant located off the lobby of the Belmont Hotel. Not so noted is the cocktail lounge, but you'll find it a quiet and comfortable place for a tryst.

Tony Barone handled the remodelling of the Tango recently, in the same chic style of his work at the Brewery and several Lettuce Entertain You places, with a wall-length couch, tables and plush chairs. Most of the drinkers here are en route to the dining room, but you can be comfortable with their liquids and the excellent hors d'oeures they provide.

The Tango's special feature is its extensive collection of rare and ancient brandies and liqueurs, and the wine list is extensive, offering over 150 wines ranging from $6.50 to $90.

Here you'll enjoy a subdued atmosphere, candlelit quiet, drinking with classical music in the background.

5pm-11 (sun), 12 (Mon), 2 (Tues-Fri), 3 (Sat), $, 85¢/$1.50, wine list, 1 dom/2 imp, no games, taped music.

There Is No Name

1334 N. Cicero   261-2218
No names given

First of all, you'll drive past it and won't believe it exists. No one seems to make it there directly or easily the first time. There Is No Name sits across from a factory wasteland on the fringe of a tiny neighborhood which is hemmed in by industry. If you've been there once, the next time you'll discover they're using a different door as an entrance. There are three doors in all and every weekend the owners choose which one to use. Then they shove pinball and bowling games around to block the other two. (Yes, this eccentricity is confirmed.) They put signs on the blocked doors and watch confused patrons bang on them. "If you can't read signs we don't need you," one of the owners told me. The interior is funky junk.

Now, what do you do with this combination? If you are the nameless owners of this place you book bands and have a music bar, and you wait for people to travel to you. Amazingly, they do. Music is performed two to four nights a week, the groups change nightly. There is no regular crowd, it changes with the music.

"We used to have another bar a few years ago and never thought of a name. So we said 'There is no name' so many times that it became a name. Then we moved here, see, and . . . "

Tiff's

160 E. Huron   787-2900
Sheraton Plaza Hotel, prop.

Tiff's is a popular off-Michigan Avenue lunch and after work spot. It is cleverly arranged so that you'd never guess that it's connected to the lobby of the Sheraton Plaza, and it's quite a comfortable place. In the new style of design you'll find a stained glass, carpeted, bricked, dark wood design which is better than most. Some of the cosy tables have stuffed chairs, which I favor, and there are open windows and plants hanging around. There's a tasty hors d'oeuvres table during the early evening hours, and you can get quick service from the limited menu which has sandwiches, soups, a salad bar and a much better chili than you'll find elsewhere in the neighborhood.

Tiff's seats 80 people and it is adjacent to the Sheraton's dining room, which offers a Continental menu. Tuesday through Saturday nights there is live piano music and the rushed lunch/after work scene changes to a subdued, intimate piano bar.

11:30-2am, $, $1.00/$1.75, 4 dom/3 imp, piano 5 nights.

The Tiny Tap

112½ N. Clinton
George Del, prop.

The Tiny Tap measures 10½ feet by 40 feet and those dimensions include the whole building. Tucked away behind the Northwestern Station, T. Tap is a "men's bar." Firemen, construction workers, and suburban commuters fill the place (which isn't difficult) and a lot of drinking, swearing, and cigar smoke fill the air. The walls are plastered with enough nudes to repulse even a low-key feminist, and the place has an aura of funky Chicago decay.

All in all, the place is a Chicago must for its size and for its audacity—that it dares to exist. It was a cigar store

65 years ago and now it's the City's smallest male chauvinist tavern. Could it be piety—closed on Sunday.

8:30am-11pm (M-Sat), ¢, 65¢/90¢, no #, 5 dom/1 imp, no games, no music.

Touch of Green

11044 S. Western Ave.   239-2992
Vince Carey & Jack Casto

The owners wanted to create a place in the style of Butch Maguire's or Shennanigan's, but they wanted to put it on the far Southwest side, to eliminate a 20 mile commute for the citizens there. To do that, you have to get Phil Rowe to design the place, and they did just that, after having been told, by Rowe, "I don't do bars on the South Side." Vince Carey re-opened the door slammed in his face, and Rowe relented.

What was once a small Mexican restaurant is now a barn-like structure with cathedral ceilings, a rectangular island bar, wooden booths and three major rooms, a testimony to Rowe's powers of metamorphosis. The usual antiques-brass-stained glass routine is spread rather thin, but that seems to be a benefit rather than a handicap, for you get a clean spacious feeling from the place. Its patrons are those Southsiders you'd expect to find in Maguire's, but who've saved themselves a trip.

There are hors d'oeuvres served from 5-7, an inexpensive sandwich/chili menu, and some bar games. Thursday nights they offer live American folk music, and occasionally Irish traditional.

11am-2, ¢, 60¢/90¢, # 5-7, 3 dom/1 imp, pinball electronic, juke & live Thurs.

2350 Pub

2249 N. Lincoln Ave.   281-9859
Charles Dee, prop.

First of all, it's *not* at 2350 N. Lincoln, it *was* at 2350 N.
Clark until, having lost a lease, the place was trans-
planted from Clark Street. Keep that in mind when
giving directions to a friend on how to meet you there.

The 2350 is a 50-50 split between bar and restaurant,
and food is the main attraction. Here, while sitting at the
bar, you can have an artichoke with drawn butter or
french fried eggplant, and sitting at a table you can be
served a full meal.

The miracle of the place is that late at night, especially
after 2am when the rest of the city turns miraculously to
grease, you can grab a good meal, and continue to drink
away at the same time. Besides the menu, which even
vegetarians find more than acceptable, you can have a
belly-ful of ice cream drinks made with Vala's ice cream.
If you have a craving for a strawberry blitz (gin, vanilla
ice cream, fresh strawberries and cream, $2.25) this is
the place to go.

The decor is pleasant and clean, the atmosphere
friendly. The 2350 drinks are made with 1½oz. of booze
and at cocktail hour the second drink costs a penny.

11am-4am-$, 65¢/$1.35, # 3-6, 2 dom/4 imp, pinball,
bowling, juke.

Twiggs

233 E. Erie   337-0380

At this writing the business is up for sale, but whoever
buys it will have to keep the interior, regardless of what
the name will be. A fellow named Paul Magaiek has
designed and installed what he calls "infinite walls." The
walls of the place are glass boxes loaded with stark,
near-white branches and backed by mirrors. You gaze
into an eerie forest without end, and the effect is strange.
There's a bar and a drinking area reserved from the
dining room, but the walls are something from a startling

science fiction world. The feeling is almost uncomfortable, museum-like in its lifelessness. Since the whole operation cost a fortune, the new owners wouldn't buy the place unless they planned to maintain, or at the most alter the place. Not for the late night drinking insomniac.

Twin Anchors

1655 N. Sedgewick   WH4-9714
Rose Gard, prop.

The Twin Anchors is a friendly comfortable neighborhood tavern in the Old Town area. It opens at 7am, serves drinks at reasonable prices and has a thriving restaurant in the rear. It used to have a seafood menu, but now it's simply ribs, chicken, steak and sandwiches. Just as pizza addicts have their "best pizza" debates, so do fans of the barbequed rib. The Twin Anchors is mentioned often in the "best ribs" debate. The place is known nationally and an occasional celebrity such as Sinatra has been known to stroll in. The design is simple; dark wood, tables, chairs and booths are present without any attempts at prettying the place up. It was, as every other near Northside place was, a speakeasy back in the Dark Ages.

7am-midnight (restaurant 4pm-midnight), ¢, 40¢/90¢, 10 dom/3 imp, bowling, juke.

Universal Liquors

3119 W. 111th St.   233-4004
Ed Beinor, prop.

The Universal is a notable dive. Notable because it is cheap, cheap, cheap. 35c for a beer. Mixed drinks 55c. Shot of Daniels 65c. Cutty Sark 75c. Located in Mount Greenwood, that white section of the city in the far southwest corner, it's a workingman's bar. Smokey, grimy, it's located in the back of a liquor store. There's nothing going on but drinking and talking.

It's a neighborhood tradition, among those who feel they can sneer, that every Sunday at 11:45am the line begins to form at the Universal. Like caged lions the drinkers pace back and forth, looking nervous, waiting for the clock to move so that the place can open. They stalk and mutter curses at whatever foolish forces made the liquor laws that prohibit drinking till noon on Sunday.

9am-11pm, 35¢/55¢, 8 dom/3 imp.

The Victorian House

800 W. Belmont
Richard Bobbitt & Al Morlock, props.

I'm not sure if it's a restaurant/bar or a museum. As a museum, it's well worth seeing. The owners spent five years designing and collecting for the place and two years to restore and assemble what they have in the site of the old 7am shot-and-beer Busy Bee tavern. The place is full to the brim with Chicago antiques from the 1890-1910 era. Since Chicago developers will swat away a mansion without hesitation, there've been a lot of incredible antiques thrown loose in the last decade.

The Victorian House has captured items from the Shedd manion, the Pullman mansion and that of Admiral Dewey. The old Marlboro, Paradise and Century theatres have also contributed. The stuff is strictly Chicago area and Victorian, and you could use a catalog to list it all. There's an amazing series of stained glass windows, Tiffany (real) lamps, antique clocks, etched glass, mirrors, etched wood, a fireplace, and a nickelodeon that will play "When the Saints Come Marching In", or "The Yellow Rose of Texas" for a quarter. The place is full of things to see.

The menu is American, with dinner prices ranging from $5 to $10. For the drinker, there's a beautiful oak bar, comfortable stools, and a half-price cocktail hour from noon till six. They have a fancy drink menu with a dozen or so cutesy items such as the Banana Ballou, dedicated to Miss Addie, who in 1917, declared Chicago to be "an evil place countenancing 350 brothels . . . a modern Sodom." I'll drink to that, but not with something made with chocolate ice cream, banana, rum, and creme de banana and de cacao all for $2.50. There's cheese and crackers served at the bar and the beer comes in frosted steins. Give the place a visit, at least for the stained glass.

11-2, $, 80¢/$1.50, # noon-6, 12 wines $4-$7, 6 dom/ 3 imp, FM.

Vogt's Wine Shop

1100 W. Adams   HA1-2875
The Vogt Family, props.

Vogt's Wine Shop is anything but a sophisticated wine mart. It's a bizarre liquor commissary, a wholesale warehouse, a wino's stopoff. Three generations of the Vogt family work behind a long counter selling every-thing from half pints and salvage wine to penny candy. The place is cavernous, filled with rows and rows of skids laden with beer, wine and soda. The building, which has housed saloons for over 100 years, is just a block off skid row. Its bar, now defunct, is a piece of Chicago history.

If you're in the mood for a little surreal slumming, drop into Vogt's for a case of something. The prices can't be beat. While you're there, pick out a can of beer from the "loose" selection in one of the open coolers, pay for it, pop a top and, following an ancient tradition, take a seat on a stack of cases and drink away. Surrounded by boxes of fresh fruit, vegetables, racks of junk food and the stacks of cases, you can take in this rare cityscape. Panhandlers, ghetto people, police, dogs and other colorful Chicagoans fill the scene. It's not for the timid.

Grandfather Vogt, who toils there daily, can tell tales of Chicago in the real turn of the century saloon days. He recalls when beer was kept in ice houses, pumped by hand, and delivered by teamsters who drove teams. Mr. Vogt warms to his subject when he remembers the politicians. "They'd come in a tavern and put twenty dollars down on the bar to buy the people a drink. Yeah, back they they'd *spend* money in a tavern. It's all turned around today. Now, we have to pay them off!"

6:30am-8pm weekdays, 10:30 weekends, cheap, no bar services.

WGAF

4001 S. Archer   523-9836
Emil Valack & Ken Oliver

"Visitation" is a Catholic church on the Southside that has spawned thousands of the city's Irish Catholics who have gone into the world to have a wide variety of careers and lifestyles, some of them admirable. WGAF ("who gives a fuck" to the cogniscenti) is the home bar for the young Irish from Visitation. The place is hip, fashionable, and more of what you would expect to find on the Near Northside or in Rogers Park. There are two rooms, the front is a simple, functional barroom and the back is reserved for games. There's a good juke box, a lot of young people, and the prices are right. They sponsor teams and have occasional special events. There's a chalkboard over the bar that tells you the economic story "mixed drinks 75c, call booze 85c, Michelob 90c, Heineken $1.00, wine 50c & 75c."

6pm-2am, Sunday noon-2, ¢, 40¢/75¢, 2 dom/1 imp, pool, foosball, bowling, pinball, juke.

Wise Fool's Pub

2270 N. Lincoln Ave.   929-1510
David Ungerleider, prop.

Wise Fool's was the first music club to bring Black musicians from their traditional haunts on the south and west sides to play for predominantly White north side audiences. Crossing the color barrier with our city's own talent, especially in the blues field, has proven to be a profitable and much imitated practice. There's a name act Wednesday through Saturday, with different groups doing one night gigs on Sunday and Tuesday.

Monday nights are reserved for Pemberton's (previously Remington's) Big Band. This has become a great Chicago jazz tradition. You can hear some of the finest big band performances in the world right there on Lincoln Avenue. Since Monday is traditionally musicians' night off, the band often welcomes an unexpected guest performer. The atmosphere is casual and comfortable, but the music room is small, so if you want to see a particular performance, come early.

4pm-2am, $, 75¢/$1.30, # 4-8, 3 dom/4 imp, pool table, live music, usually blues, jazz and other in that order, cover varies, 2 drink min., performances at 9:45, Mondays start earlier.

The Wrigley Bar

410 N. Michigan   WH4-7600
Wrigley Corp., prop.

Tucked away in the rear of the ground floor of the Wrigley Building is the Wrigley restaurant and bar. It's as old and traditional as the rest of the Wrigley empire in Chicago. It belongs to the generation of folks who are in their 50's now, with its padded vinyl booths and bartenders in vests. The bar is curved, the atmosphere is civilized, and its patrons are any of the folk who work on the magnificent mile.

11am-7pm.

Z Sports Tap

1139 N. Dearborn
Earle Zimmerman, prop.

"A neighborhood bar in the jungle," that's how Earle Zimmerman describes his place. Smack in the middle of the Rush Street slick scene, hidden inside what was someone's elegant home 90 years ago, you can find Z Sports Tap. What was the living room now looks like a living room filled with tables and chairs. There's a wood burning fireplace and large windows. The bar runs across the back wall of the building, and the washrooms are up a curved staircase.

Neighborhood bar activities go on here. The TV gives you "the game," whichever one is on, pinball is played, people know each other and carry the banter back and forth, and Earle conducts his business in the fine tradition of the tavern host. So, if you're walking around the jungle and see a sign advertising Z Sports Tap half a flight up on the front of an unlikely building, walk in and join the neighborhood crowd.

3pm-2, $, 70¢/$1.25, # 4-8, 1 dom/o imp, games, oldies juke.

Zum Deutschen Eck

2924 N. Southport   525-8121
Al Wirth, prop.

At the confluence of the Rhine and Moselle Rivers there is a monument celebrating the coronation of Kaiser Wilhelm I in 1870. The land in the angle created by the rivers is the "German Corner." Many inns up and down the Rhine are named Zum Deutchen Eck, which means "at the German corner." Al Wirth thought this was quite a nifty name for his place back in 1955, until he realized it put him last in the telephone listing of German restaurants. The building is big and inn-like, and it's 110 years old. It was Weber's Hall and alderman Charlie Weber was born upstairs. Now it's a fully decorated Germanic inn, with a large rectangular bar that will seat many thirsty souls. The beams above the bar are hung with dozens of those ceramic steins and other appropriate knick knacks. Beer is served in quarter liter, half liter or full liter steins, and glass boots are available for the suicidal beer drinker. There's a nice selection of wines and beers to be had, and the place fills up on weekends in beer hall style with enthusiastic sing-alongs with Hans and Danny. I can offer one small consolation to Mr. Wirth; in this book Zum Deutschen Eck appears before Zum Lieben Augustin.

Mon-Fri 3pm-1am, Sat noon-3am, Sun noon-1am, $, 65¢/$1.10, 22 wines $5.75-$10, 5 dom/12 imp, pinball, music Fri-Sun 7pm-1am.

Zum Lieben Augustin

4600 N. Lincoln Ave.   334-2919
Jochen Ettel, prop.

Zum L. A. is dedicated "to lovable Augustin," some half-forgotten hero of a fable from the German middle ages. Here you'll find "schunken," where everyone, from table to table, links arms and sways back and forth to live music. There's dancing as well, a nice German menu, and some imported beers to sample.

Zum L. A. is the first bar in the city to carry Hacker-pschon Munchneralt, a dark, yeasty beer similar to weissbier, which must be kept refrigerated in its transit from Germany.

The specialty menu is very reasonable, with plate dinners ranging from $1.50 to $4.50, and it fits well with the general cabaret atmosphere. There are fake grapes hanging about, curtains, carpeting, and a semi-garden feeling to it. So, starting at 8:30, every night of the week, the live music begins. Get ready for the "schunken."

11am-2, $, 65¢/$1.00, 15 wines $7/$15, 1 dom/9 imp, live European music 7 nights.

248-7325

Geographic Index

This index will give you a general guide to bars located in the same geographic areas. Boundaries can be vague, and they often overlap.

Downtown—This is the center of the city, known often as the Loop, an area circled by the Lake Street L tracks. It's primarily a 9-to-5 business district, with lots of cafeteria style (regardless of the decor) drinking. Office folk, business suits, shoppers, and an 8pm evacuation are the general rules for drinkers.

Barney's Market Club
Bar RR
Barton's
The Baton
The Berghoff Cafe
The Bistro (Dugan's)
Cafe Bohemia
The Gold Coast
Hobson's

Joann
King Arthur's Pub
Marina Ship's Bar
Mirage
Old Polonia (aka Warsaw Cafe)
Rick's Cafe Americain
Sign of the Trader
The Tiny Tap

On or Off North Michigan Avenue—North of the Downtown area you'll find the Magnificent Mile of Chicago's front yard. It's here that the Chicago advertising, newspaper, photo and film industry goes on. The drinking is appropriately fashion and image conscious.

Bar of the Ritz
Billy Goat Tavern
Boccaccio's
Boul Mich
The Brassary
Cape Cod Room
Coq d'Or
Great Gritzbe's
Greenhouse
Hogan's
Lawry's
Lion Bar

The Lobby Bar
Meson del Lago
Mrs. O'Leary's
The 1944 St. Louis Browns
Playboy Club
Riccardo's
Sage's East
Sherlock's Home
Sybaris Lounge
Tiff's
Twigg's
Wrigley Restaurant Bar

The Rush Street Area—The North Michigan Avenue section runs into the Rush Street area, which is the central strip for visitors to the city who "want action." There's an incredible range of places here, including hidden working men's bars, strip-clip joints that don't serve liquor, great music bars, perhaps the strongest "singles" scene on the continent, ritzy lounges, high fashion private clubs, discos, and rock and roll hellholes. This is a hard part of town for the stranger. It's possible to wander around from place to place, spending a fortune and not having a good time, so caveat emptor.

The Acorn	Harry's Cafe
Adolph's	The Hotsie Totsie Club
Arnie's &	Jim Gorman's
Arnie's Sidewalk Cafe	Melvin's
Alfie's	Mister Joe's
The Back Room	Mon Petit
The Barbarossa	Mother's
The BBC	Muldoon's Saloon
Booze & Bits	(see Jim Gorman's)
Butch McGuire's	O'Leary's
The Domino	Patrice
The Embers	Pippin's
The Embers	The Pump Room
Eugene's	She-nannigans
Figaro's	Sweetwater
Finley's	The Terrace
The Hange Uppe	Z Sports Tap

Near North—This is a general phrase I'll use to include places from North Avenue (1600 N.) to Belmont (3200 N.) near the lake. It includes Old Town, Lincoln Park and New Town, but since the bars are often on the borderline, I've lumped them together. Generally, Old Town is a tourist pit that is best avoided, though it has a few saving graces listed below. Lincoln Park has the city's young, liberal, occasionally bohemian drinking scene, and New Town includes the "gay Ghetto" and a strong singles scene. Newcomers to the city who can't take the pace or style of Rush Street will do well to migrate a little further North to investigate these regions.

The Bar Association
Beowulf
Best Wines and Liquors
Black Forest
Blue and Gold
The Brewery
The Brownstone
The Bulls
The Clark Street Cafe
Colette's
The Como Inn
Durkin's
The Earl of Old Town
Elsewhere
The Fat Black Pussycat
Flannagan's
Frere Jacques
Gaffer's
Gaslight Corner
Geja's
Germania Inn
The Golden Ox
Hashikin
Jasper's
John Barleycorn
   Memorial Pub
Kelly's
La Mere Vipere
Marge's

Martingayle's
Mickey's
Mister Kiley's
Nick's
Northbranch Saloon
Old Town Ale House
O'Rourke's
Orsi's
Otto's
Oxford
Papa John's
Park West
The Quiet Night
Redford's
The River Shannon
The Rusty Scupper
Second City
Shari's
Single File
The Skyline
Somebody Else's Troubles
Sterch's
Sylvester's
Tango
The 2350 Pub
Twin Anchors
The Victorian House
Wise Fools Pub

Farther North—This includes all of the area north and west, from the near north area, to the city limits. This is a large "neighborhood" chunk of Chicago with a variety of drinking environments.

Baron's Disco & Lounge
Biddy Mulligan's
Broadway Joe's
Cabaret Act 2
Chicago Club of the Deaf
Clearwater Saloon

Cubby-Bear Restaurant
   and Lounge
The Crown Pub
Cunneen's
Disco, Act 1
Gaspar's

The Ginger Man
Glenshesk
Grover's Oyster Bar
Hamilton's
Hogen's
Leo's Southport Lanes
Lutz's
Michel's
Miomir's
Moody's Pub
Moose's Lounge
New York Lounge
North Center Bowl
O'Hare Airport
   International Lounge
O'Shaughnessey's

Pam's Playhouse
The Portside
The Pumping Company
Ray's Bleachers
Rese's Bierstube
Sam's Working Man's
   Palace
Schulein's
Scott's
The Slammer Inn
Slowik's
The Swiss Inn
The Tally-Ho Lounge
Unameit
Zum Deutchen Eck
Zum Lieben Augustin

West Side—This includes the areas due west of downtown, to the city limits. It, too, is a "neighborhood" section of Chicago.

Bucket o' Suds
   (aka Joe Danno's)
Durty Dick's
Ile de France
The Irish Village
La Concha

Little Joe's
Ragtime Inn
Smiler Coogan's
There Is No Name
Vernon Park Tap
Vogt's Wine Shop

The Southside—This is a vast geographic category, which includes all of the territory to the southern city limits. It includes the like of Mayor Daley's Bridgeport, the little-known Eastside, Marquette Park, and the nearly suburban strip way down at 111th Street. Many Chicagoans have never been to the Southside, and many don't want to go. It's the area where neighborhoods are neighborhoods.

The Baby Doll Polka
   Lounge
Checkerboard Lounge
The Celtic Lounge

Erik the Red
Gavin's
The Golden Shell
The Import Tap

Knight's Inn
Lindy's
The Midget Club
The Marquis
Poor Men's Pub
Schaller's
Sheahon's

Sonny's Inn
Sorrento's
Shinnick's
Touch of Green
Universal Liquors
WGAF

Hyde Park—This is the Southside island community which circles the University of Chicago.

The Cove
Cornell Restaurant
The Eagle Pub

Jimmy's (aka The
  Woodlawn Tap)
The Tiki

Features Index

This is an index of Chicago bars by type. Of course the designations are capricious and dictated by my whimsical fancy, so don't trust them altogether. There are ethnic bars that are also neighborhood taverns, for example, and the distinction between young people's bars and singles bars is still a little vague in my mind. I think it's that singles bars have a dress code, while young people's bars welcome the blue-jeaned, bohemians and slobs, regardless of their age. The line between a dash of elegance and the classics is also a bit confused at times, although I believe that the classics have years as well as elegance behind them. At any rate, you must realize that the index is the last part of this book, and the author has suffered, for your benefit, occasional bouts of cerebral distortion, yea, perhaps permanent brain damage, in his struggle to complete it.

The Classics
The Acorn
Adolph's
Barney's Market Club
The Berghoff Cafe
Best Wines and Liquors
Billy Goat Tavern
Boul Mich
Como Inn
The Coq d'Or
Joann
The Golden Ox
The Playboy Club
Riccardo's
Schaller's
The Wrigley Restaurant
    Bar

For a Dash of Elegance
Arnie's
Barton's
Geja's

The Greenhouse
Lawry's
Patrice
The Pump Room
Tango
The Terrace

Dives
Tiki
Ray's Bleachers
Sam's Working Man's
    Palace
Universal Liquors
Unameit
Vogt's Wine Shop

Ethnic Bars
Black Forest
Germania Inn
Golden Shell
Little Joe's
La Concha

The Old Polonia
Resi's Bierstube
Slowik's
The Swiss Inn
Vernon Park Tap
Zum Deutchen Eck
Zum lieben Augustin

Food Bars

Boccaccio's
Cape Cod Room
The Cove
Great Gritzbe's
Grover's Oyster Bar
Hobson's
Hogen's
John Barleycorn
   Memorial Pub
Lindy's
Lutz's
Martingayle's
Melvin's
Meson del Lago
Moody's Pub
Mrs. O'Leary's
Otto's
The Portside
Tiff's
The 2350 Pub
Twin Anchors
The Victorian House

Gay Bars

Alfie's
The Brownstone
Cabaret, Act 2
Disco, Act 1
The Gold Coast
Shari's
Women's Gay Bars

Music Bars

Baron's Disco & Lounge
The Baby Doll
   Polka Lounge
The Back Room
The Barbarossa
Bar of the Ritz
Biddy Mulligan's
The Bull's
Checkerboard Lounge
Clearwater Saloon
Colette's
Durty Dick's
The Earl of Old Town
Elsewhere
Gaspar's
Glenshesk
The Irish Village
The Marquis
Miomir's
Mister Kiley's
Moose's Lounge
Northbranch Saloon
Pam's Playhouse
Park West
The Quiet Night
Redford's
Rick's Cafe Americain
Scott's
The Single File
The Skyline
Somebody Else's Troubles
There is No Name
Wise Fools Pub

Neighborhood Taverns

Blue & Gold
Broadway Joe's
The Celtic Lounge
Cornell Restaurant
The Eagle Pub
Gaslight Corner
The Ginger MAn

Import Tap
Hogan's
Jimmy's (aka Woodlawn
 Tap)
Marge's
Michel's
Mickey's
Mister Joe's
Old Town Ale House
O'Rourke's
Papa John's
Poor Man's Pub
Ragtime Inn
Smiler Coogan's
Sonny's Inn
Sterch's
Tally-Ho Lounge
Z Sports Tap

One of a Kind

Bar RR
The Baton
Booze & Bits
Chicago Club of the Deaf
Cubby-Bear Restaurant
 & Lounge
Bucket o'Suds (Joe
 Danno's)
The Domino
Figaro's
Hashikin
Le Mere Vipere
Leo's Southport Lanes
Marina Ship's Bar
The Midget Club
Mirage
New York Lounge
The 1944 St. Louis Browns
North Center Bowl
O'Hare Airport Inter-
 national Lounge
Oxford Pub
Sign of the Trader
The Slammer Inn

The Sybaris Lounge
Second City
Sylvester's
The Tiny Tap

Singles Bars

BBC
Brassary
Butch McGuire's
Brewery
Clark Street Cafe
Durkin's
Finley's
Flannagan's
Gaffer's
Hange Uppe
Harry's Cafe
Hotsie Totsie Club
Jaspar's
Jim Gorman's
Mother's
Muldoon's Saloon
 (see Jim Gorman's)
O'Leary's
She-nannigans
Sweetwater
River Shannon
Rusty Scupper
Touch of Green

Young Peoples' Hangouts

Beowulf
Cunneen's
Erik the Red
Fat Black Pussycat
Gavin's
Hamilton's
Kelly's
Nick's
O'Shaughnessey's
Pippin's
Pumping Company
Sheahon's

Shinnick's
WGAF

Retreats
Bar Association
Cafe Bohemia
Crown Pub, O'Hare
The Embers
Eugene's
Frere Jacques
Ile de France

King Arthur's
The Knight's Inn
The Lion Bar
The Lobby Bar
Mon Petit
Orsi's
Sage's East
Schulein's
Sherlock's Home
Sorrento's
Twiggs

Acc H